REAL GRAMMAR

A Corpus-Based Approach to English

Susan Conrad

Douglas Biber

With activities contributed by
Kate Daly
Sara Packer

PEARSON
Longman

Real Grammar:
A Corpus-Based Approach to English

Pearson Education, 10 Bank Street, White Plains, NY 10606

Staff credits: The people who made up the *Real Grammar* team,
representing editorial, production, design, and manufacturing
are: Pietro Alongi, Rhea Banker, Rosa Chapinal, Dave Dickey,
Françoise Leffler, Jaime Lieber, Linda Moser, Massimo Rubini,
Jennifer Stem, and Paula Van Ells.

Cover design: Carie Keller, Nesbitt Graphics, Inc.
Text design and composition: Nesbitt Graphics, Inc.
Text font: 10.5/12 Minion

Library of Congress Cataloging-in-Publication Data

Conrad, Susan.
  Real grammar : a corpus-based approach to English / Susan Conrad,
Douglas Biber ; with activities contributed by Kate Daly, Sara Packer.
    p. cm.
  ISBN-10: 0-13-515587-8
  ISBN-13: 978-0-13-515587-5
  1. English language—Grammar. I. Biber, Douglas. II. Daly, Kate.
III. Packer, Sara. IV. Title.
  PE1112.C636 2009
  425—dc22
                            2009018615

Printed in the United States of America
2 3 4 5 6 7 8 9 10–V016–15 14 13 12 11 10

Contents

A New Kind of Grammar Book

Real Grammar: A Corpus-Based Approach to English is new in many ways.

- **It is based on a corpus.** A corpus is a very large collection of spoken and written texts. We used computers to analyze the Longman Corpus Network to see how people really speak and write, so *Real Grammar* can help you learn authentic English grammar.

- **It is a supplement.** We know that you have studied basic grammar in a traditional textbook. This supplement will teach you more specific information, especially how speakers and writers actually use grammar. You will even learn more about "easy" grammar structures.

- **It focuses on typical grammar.** *Real Grammar* looks at the grammatical patterns that are most common in speech or writing. You may have heard people label grammar as "correct" or "incorrect." But some "correct" structures just aren't used in certain circumstances. Using English proficiently means knowing typical grammar in addition to correct grammar.

- **It covers different grammar choices for speech and writing.** Using grammar appropriately means making the right choice for a casual conversation vs. an academic paper. This book will help you to learn the grammar that is typical in conversation, and how that is different from the grammar typical in writing.

- **It presents grammar with connections to vocabulary.** Many grammatical structures are commonly used with certain words. *Real Grammar* identifies the words that most frequently occur with each grammatical structure.

- **It uses authentic language examples.** Only language that was spoken or written by real people in natural situations appears here. No examples were created just for this book!

- **It presents grammar structures in a discourse context.** That means you see the grammar with other natural language around it.

- **It helps you to understand grammar in reading and listening, besides using it in speaking and writing.** Understanding the grammar others use is as important as producing it yourself. *Real Grammar* has activities to make you think about how grammar is used and what it means.

Using the Book

Real Grammar has 50 units, organized into 11 parts. The units are organized in a logical sequence, with more difficult units toward the end of the parts. However, each unit is complete on its own. This means you can work on units in any order you choose. You can also choose to focus on only conversation or writing; the speech and/or writing icons next to the title of each unit will help you make your selection.

If you are in a grammar class, you can match the topics of units to your traditional grammar book and use the units to supplement your traditional book. Alternatively, especially if you are an advanced student of English, you can work through this book independently in order to refine your grammar skills.

Using the Units

Each unit heading in *Real Grammar* has **three types of information:**

- The **language title** shows an example of the target structure, taken from the corpus:
  It really made a difference . . .

- The **grammar title** describes the target structure: Meanings of *Make* + Noun Phrase

- **Icons** show whether the structure is common in **conversation, writing, or both.** The words "Academic Writing" or "Informational Writing" appear under the writing icon if the unit focuses especially on those kinds of writing.

Each unit of *Real Grammar* has three pages, composed of **three sections:**

➤ **What have you learned from your grammar textbook?**

This short background section covers what you should already know about the target structure. If this information is not familiar, go back to your traditional grammar textbook and review it.

➤ **What does the corpus show?**

This section presents findings from research on the corpus. This information might contradict something in your traditional textbook. It might add more specific information. It might surprise you, or it might explain things you've heard in real conversations. In most units, *Frequency Information* tells you what items are common with a grammar structure. All the information is **based on research with the corpus.** Some units have *Be careful!* points that emphasize how to avoid typical errors or confusion.

➤ **Activities**

Each unit has activities sequenced to help you understand and then use the target structure.

- *Noticing* **activities** are first. These simple exercises draw your attention to the structure in a discourse context and help you to examine more examples of how it is used.

- *Analysis* **activities** ask you to do things like identify the names of structures, correct errors in learners' writing, and distinguish among meanings or functions. By analyzing a structure, you will come to understand it better.

- *Practice* **activities** ask you to use the target structure in speaking or writing.

You will find a complete **Answer Key** for these activities on the following website:
http://www.pearsonlongman.com/realgrammar

Terms Used in This Book

corpus a large, carefully designed collection of spoken and written texts, analyzed with the help of computers, and used for studying language

register a type of language used for a specific purpose in a specific situation. The four main registers in this book are conversation, fiction, newspaper, and academic writing:

- **conversation** (CONV.) talk between two or more people
- **fiction** (FICT.) writing in novels and short stories
- **newspaper** (NEWS) writing in newspapers
- **academic writing** (ACAD.) writing in textbooks, journal articles, and technical books

informational writing writing whose main purpose is to convey information. It is sometimes called "expository writing." In this book, informational writing includes newspaper and academic writing.

discourse written or spoken communication

text a section of discourse, such as several sentences from a book or part of a conversation. A text can also be a complete written document, such as a newspaper article or a book.

context the words and sentences that come before or after the structure that you are studying. Context can also mean the situation — for example, is communication spoken or written? Are the speakers friends or strangers? What is the purpose of the communication? Context helps people understand language and make appropriate language choices when they speak or write.

icons small signs or pictures indicating that the target structures are common in the following registers:

 conversation

 writing

 academic writing

newspaper and academic writing

Remember, *Real Grammar* focuses on typical grammar—the grammatical patterns that are most common in speech and writing. For teachers who have previously focused on correctness, this will be a new approach. But learners have to handle issues related to appropriateness, not just correctness, every time they speak and write. Most learners want to know how native speakers most typically choose to say or write something. Now that corpus research has shown us the typical choices, there is no reason to keep this information a secret!

The corpus findings, especially *Frequency Information*, may not be consistent with your intuition. Corpus research has shown that we often are not consciously aware of the most common language choices we make. Rest assured that the information in this book is based on principled analysis of a large, carefully designed corpus. For further details about the findings, you can consult the *Longman Grammar of Spoken and Written English* or the *Longman Student Grammar of Spoken and Written English* (see Suggested Titles below).

All of the examples and all of the items in the activities are taken from the corpus so that students see grammatical structures as they were used by native speakers. At the same time, it is important for the language of the corpus extracts not to overwhelm students or to take their attention away from the structure that is being practiced. If it was necessary, we modified corpus extracts in limited ways to make them more accessible to students. We permitted **only a small number of modifications:**

- Difficult vocabulary was changed to easier vocabulary, using the same part of speech.

- Sentences that were extremely long and complex were simplified by deleting optional elements (e.g., optional adverbials).

- In discourse passages of academic writing, some intervening sentences were deleted while retaining the context and the target structures.

- In conversation, excessive fillers and false starts were reduced. A reasonable number were retained in order to maintain the "flavor" of conversation.

- In conversation, non-standard syntax that was likely to impede comprehension was standardized slightly, for example, by adding punctuation.

SUGGESTED TITLES		
Longman Grammar of Spoken and Written English		
	0-582-23725-4	978-0-582-23725-4
Longman Student Grammar of Spoken and Written English		
Student Book	0-582-23727-2	978-0-582-23727-8
Workbook	0-582-53942-0	978-0-582-53942-6

Acknowledgments

Real Grammar has benefited from the input of numerous people. We would especially like to thank the teachers who piloted units in their classrooms and provided helpful feedback: Darbra Smith, Heather De Munn, YouJin Kim, and Norman Yoshida. Thanks also to the Portland State University Corpus Group and to the many students and teachers in Arizona, Oregon, and throughout the world who gave us feedback on earlier versions of units, the table of contents, and other matters. Finally, we have been very fortunate to work with Françoise Leffler as our editor at Pearson Longman; her expertise improved both the book itself and the process of its production.

Susan Conrad and Douglas Biber

Reviewers and Piloters

The publisher would like to thank the following reviewers and piloters for their valuable comments and insights.

Linda Anderson, Washington University; **Eric Arbogast**, Westchester Community College; **Kim Bayer**, Hunter College; **Kathleen Belitsky**, Mt Wachusett Community College; **Diane Bumpass**, Virginia Commonwealth University; **Linda Butler**, Holyoke Community College; **Sharon Cavusgil**, Georgia State University; **Nancy Centers**, Roger Williams University; **Christopher Davis**, Hunter College; **Heather De Munn**, Keimyung University; **Kaye Foster**, Sierra College; **Anthony Halderman**, Cuesta College; **Mary Hill**, North Shore Community College; **Barbara Hockman**, CCSF, San Francisco; **Tamara Jones**, Howard Community College; **Mandy Kama**, Georgetown; **Gwendolyn Kane**, Raritan Valley Community College; **YouJin Kim**, Northern Arizona University; **Katie Leite**, Howard Community College; **Kathy Mills-Hastings**, Westchester Community College; **Tom Riedmiller**, University of Northern Iowa; **Sarah Saxer**, Howard Community College; **Kathy Sherak**, SFSU, San Francisco; **Darbra Smith**, Portland State University; **Michelle Smith**, Bunker Hill Community College; **Helen Solórzano**, Suffolk University; **Marjorie Stamberg**, Hunter College; **Margery Toll**, CSU Fresno; **Gita Villensky**, Miami-Dade College; **Carol Wilson-Duffy**, Michigan State University; **Norman Yoshida**, Lewis and Clark College

Did you want more coffee?
Simple Past Tense in Polite Offers

What have you learned from your grammar textbook?

The **simple past tense** is used for (1) **actions**, (2) **states**, and (3) **situations** that happened **in the past** and are **finished**:

1. I *traveled* to Hawaii last year.
2. He *was* a writer.
3. —*Did* you *have* a good weekend?
   —No, we *didn't*.

What does the corpus show?

A In conversation, sometimes people use the **simple past** of *want* or *need* in order to **make an offer** or **ask someone's preference**. Questions are formed with *did + want/need*, but they refer to the **present time**:

- *Did* you *want* more coffee? [Waiter asking a customer.]
- *Did* you *need* your receipt? [Clerk asking a customer.]

In these questions, using the **simple past** is a way of being **less direct**. Therefore, *did you want/need* sounds **more polite** than *do you want/need*. Even some good friends use the polite form with each other.

NOTE: *Would you like* is also commonly used to make polite offers:
- *Would you like* more coffee?

B **Answers** to these questions are usually **NOT in the simple past**. They can be in the **simple present**, **present progressive**, or **future**, or a simple answer may have **no verb**:

Tense of Answer	Example	
1. simple present	WAITER:	*Did* you *need* milk or cream for your coffee?
	CUSTOMER:	No, I'm fine.*
2. present progressive	JOSE:	*Did* you *want* to go to a movie?
	SALLY:	Uh-uh. I'm reading a book.
3. future	YUJI:	*Did* you *want* to try one of these drinks?
	GEORGE:	Yeah, I'll have one.
4. no verb	KATHY:	*Did* you *want* chocolate on top of those?
	HASSAN:	**No thanks.**

* When saying "No" to an offer, Americans often say, "I'm fine," meaning "I'm fine without that."

C Often, **only the first offer** in a conversation is in the **simple past**. **Later offers** are in the **simple present**:

THERESE: Nancy, *did* you *want* pie?
NANCY: Yes, sure.
THERESE: **Do** you **want** cake, too?
NANCY: No, I'll try the pie this time.

WAITER: *Did* you *want* that right away or **do** you **want** to wait for your meal?
CUSTOMER: No, we'll wait for the meal.

D **Be careful!** Do **NOT use the simple past** if you are **asking for information**, not making an offer:

- **Do** you **want** to play the clarinet?   **NOT:** ~~*Did* you *want* to play the clarinet?~~

Activities

1   **Notice in context:**   Read the conversations. Underline each **_did_ + verb** that is an offer. Circle the verb in the answer. (If there is more than one verb in the offer or answer, underline or circle both verbs.)

    1. *In a store.*

         CLERK: Did you want this receipt in the bag?

      CUSTOMER: Ah yeah, that'll be fine.

         CLERK: There you go. Thank you.

    2. *Friends visiting.*

         JOHN: Did you want any tea?

        ANISA: No, I'm fine thank you.

    3. *Making evening plans.*

       MANUEL: Well, did you want to eat first before you walk, or do you want to walk and then come back and eat?

        SALLY: Oh, uh, I just need to finish writing this email, then I'll go for a walk.

    4. *In a store.*

         CLERK: Did you need a bag for this at all or . . .

      CUSTOMER: Uh no it's okay.

2   **Analyze discourse:**   Look back at Activity 1 and at the verbs you circled. Write the tense of each one of these verbs in the margin. Draw an arrow between the verb and its tense.

3   **Practice conversation:**   Complete the first conversation. Then write conversations for the situations in 2 and 3. In each conversation, make an offer or ask about preferences, and create an appropriate answer. When you are finished, practice the conversations with a partner.

    1. Maria and Luciana ask for water in a restaurant. Maria wants ice. Luciana does not.

        WAITER: Can I get you something to drink?

        MARIA: I'd like to start with water, please.

     LUCIANA: Me too.

        WAITER: Okay. **Did** you **want** it with ice?

        MARIA: _____

     LUCIANA: _____

    2. Lisa asks Anna if she needs a ride home after tennis practice, but Anna's friend Kirby is supposed to pick her up.

         LISA: _____

                 _____

        ANNA: _____

                 _____

3. Philip asks Juan if he wants more chocolate. Juan loves chocolate and has some. Philip then offers him some peanuts, but Juan does not want any.

PHILIP: _____

_____

JUAN: _____

_____

PHILIP: _____

_____

JUAN: _____

_____

4 **Practice conversation:** Invent a situation in which one person makes an offer to another person or asks what that person's preferences are. Then write a conversation for it. When you are finished, practice the conversation with a partner.

Situation:

_____

_____

Conversation:

A: _____

_____

B: _____

_____

A: _____

_____

B: _____

_____

He's looking at me . . .
Progressive Verbs vs. Simple Verbs

What have you learned from your grammar textbook?

The **progressive tenses** describe actions that are in progress:

> • This week I'**m working** on my term paper, but next week I'**ll be relaxing** at the beach.

Non-action verbs are NOT used in the progressive tenses:

> • **Do** you **want** some more cake?   NOT: ~~Are you wanting some more cake?~~

What does the corpus show?

A In general, we use **simple verbs** much more than progressive verbs:

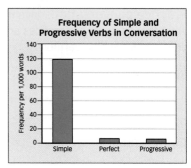

> • I **think** we **are** almost there.
> • I could **hold** that book for you.
> • I **want to go** to the library and **get** them.
> • **Remember** when you **tried to do** that?
> • I'**ll do** anything you **say**.

B In **conversation**, many different verbs **occur in the progressive**. These include both **action and non-action verbs**. Here are a few examples of such verbs:

Action Verbs Common in the Progressive			Non-Action Verbs Common in the Progressive		
bringing	*coming*	*joking*	*feeling*	*looking*	*watching*
buying	*driving*	*laughing*	*hoping*	*sitting*	*wondering*
carrying	*eating*	*talking*	*listening*	*waiting*	

Be careful! Other verbs **almost never occur in the progressive**. These also include both **action and non-action** verbs. Here are a few examples of such verbs:

Action Verbs Rare in the Progressive			Non-Action Verbs Rare in the Progressive		
convince	*reply*	*swallow*	*agree*	*hear*	*see*
find	*shut*	*thank*	*believe*	*know*	*want*
promise	*smash*	*throw*	*conclude*	*like*	

C A verb usually has **two characteristics** if it is used in the **progressive**:

1. The **subject** of the verb actively **controls** the action or state.
2. The verb describes an action or state that happens over an **extended period of time**.

> • **Are** you **listening** to that song?
> • So I **was** just **wondering** if you were offended by that.

D If a verb does **NOT have both of these characteristics**, the progressive is rare. So, if the **subject** of the verb simply "**experiences**" the action or state, the verb is in a **simple tense** (even if it describes an action or state that happens over an extended period of time):

> • She **didn't hear** him.

And if the action of the verb happens at a **single point in time**, the verb is in a **simple tense** (even if the subject of the verb actively controls the action or state):

- They **shut** the doors behind them.

E **Frequency information.** Some verbs **usually occur in the progressive** rather than in the simple tenses:

bleeding	*dripping*	*looking forward to*	*pounding*	*starving*	*sweating*
chasing	*heading for*	*lurking*	*raining*	*streaming*	*talking*
chatting	*joking*	*marching*	*screaming*	*studying*	
dancing	*kidding*	*moaning*	*shopping*		

- That's about one cup – You**'re dripping** on the floor!
- I think it was hotter today – I **was sweating** all day.

Two verbs are especially common with the **past progressive** in conversation: *was saying* and *was thinking*:

- So she **was saying** that she thought tennis would be better.
- I **was thinking** about bringing hiking boots, but they are so heavy.

Activities

1 **Notice in context:** Read each conversation, paying special attention to the boldfaced verbs. Then answer the question that follows.

1. *In the car.*

BROTHER: We're almost home.
SISTER: You **were driving** pretty slow the whole time. I can't believe it's already been an hour.
BROTHER: The time goes by so fast.
SISTER: I **promised** Mom we would be there between two and two thirty.

Which of the boldfaced verbs shows the following?

a. an action that happens over a period of time _____

b. an action that happens at one point in time _____

2. *Preparing for a trip to Hawaii.*

SARAI: Did you guys go shopping?
MANDY: Oh, no. I decided not to. I **found** some summer clothes in the back of my closet.
SARAI: Mandy, **do** you **see** my black . . . or my blue pants?
MANDY: Is this what you **are looking** for?
SARAI: No. Sweats. Pants.
MANDY: You **are bringing** four pair of sweat pants to Hawaii?
SARAI: I don't know.
MANDY: You're gonna **be carrying** a lot of luggage.
SARAI: I hope I can **shut** my suitcase.

Which of the boldfaced verbs show the following?

a. an action that is actively controlled by the subject _____

b. a state or action that is only "experienced" by the subject _____

2 **Analyze discourse:** Look at the boldfaced verbs in these conversations. If the verb is in the correct tense, write **C** on the line. If the verb is not in the correct tense, cross it out and write the correct form of the verb on the line.

1. *Before a class.*

   EMILY: Hi, Beth. A boy from your class **was wanting** to know about _____ *wanted*

   the homework, but Sam said he **found** somebody else to call. _____

   BETH: I still can't believe I **was missing** class today. _____

2. *Explaining a wedding tradition.*

   NARA: It's a Native American tradition to give presents to other

   people at a wedding. It's called a give-away.

   SULIM: Okay. 'Cause I **wondered**, since Carol and Paul **were** in the store _____

   buying all those gifts a couple of weeks ago, and I thought they _____

   shopped early for Christmas or something. _____

3. *Should we eat out?*

   KATIE: **Do** we **eat** in a restaurant tonight? _____

   DAWN: I don't know. **Are** you **looking forward to** cooking something? _____

   KATIE: Not really. You can easily **be convincing** me to eat out. _____

   DAWN: I **listened** to that radio restaurant critic, and she recommended _____

   the little Vietnamese place on Broadway.

3 **Practice conversation:** Imagine you are writing the script for a movie. Complete the scene with dialogue and stage directions (what the characters do in the scene). Include at least five more simple verbs and five more progressive verbs, and underline these verbs as you write them. When you are finished, practice the scene with a partner.

Scene: *Jay has just landed on an island after his ship wrecked in a storm. He hears someone cough on the other side of the small island.*

   JAY: Hey! [He <u>is waving</u> his arms in the air and <u>shouting</u>.] Hey! How long have you been here?

   JIM: Oh! What? [Jim <u>stands</u> up, confused.] I <u>guess</u> I <u>was watching</u> so carefully for ships that I

   <u>didn't</u> even <u>notice</u> you. How <u>did</u> you <u>get</u> here?

   JAY: Well . . . _____

   _____

   JIM: _____

   _____

   JAY: _____

   _____

   JIM: _____

   _____

UNIT 3

Studies have shown . . .
Discovery Verbs and Existence Verbs

Academic Writing

What have you learned from your grammar textbook?

The **present perfect tense** is used for actions or states that happened or **started at an unspecified time in the past**. The action or state **continues into the present** or is still important in the present.

- He *has written* extensively about foreign affairs.
- The gap between rich and poor *has widened*.

What does the corpus show?

A In academic writing, "discovery verbs" such as *discover, find,* and *show* are often used in the **present perfect tense**. These verbs tell the results of past research or studies, and they emphasize that the results **continue to be important or relevant**:

- Researchers *have discovered* how important relationships are with both colleagues and students.
- The International Labor Office *has found* this to be an international trend.
- Experiments *have shown* that plants can maintain rapid growth.

B **Discovery verbs** can also occur in the **simple present tense** and **simple past tense** in academic writing. Discovery verbs in the **simple present** tense emphasize that results are **currently true**:

- Moorat's study *shows* that older patients are especially prone to accidents.

In the **simple past** tense, these verbs suggest that the findings are **not as important or relevant now**:

- A research survey in 1986/87 *showed* that pupils frequently had no textbooks.

C Another kind of verb is also common in academic writing: "existence verbs" such as *represent* and *consist of*. Existence verbs usually **do NOT occur in the present perfect**. These verbs usually occur in the **simple present tense**. They describe a current state or logical relationship.

- Our alphabetic writing system *represents* the sounds of speech. [**NOT** ~~has represented~~]
- The rice in the field *consists of* plants of different types. [**NOT** ~~has consisted of~~]

D **Frequency information.** Here are lists of some of the **most common discovery verbs and existence verbs** used in academic writing:

Common Discovery Verbs (Frequently in the Present Perfect)		Common Existence Verbs (Usually NOT in the Present Perfect)	
have discovered		comprise	denote
have found		consist of	depend on
have revealed		constitute	illustrate
have shown		contain	include
have uncovered		correspond	represent

- Studies of solidified lava flows *have revealed* evidence of many magnetic reversals.
- Subsequent work by Barron (1988) *has shown* that the oyster mushroom can utilize bacterial colonies.

- The Colville Lake community *consists of* seventy-five members of the Hare Indians.
- The accounts now *contain* the complete salary information for the month.

Activities

1 **Notice in context:** Read this paragraph from an academic text about research on neighborhoods. Circle the "discovery verbs" and underline the "existence verbs."

Despite problems, some researchers have discovered residents' feelings about their neighborhoods by using questionnaires. Pacione (1984) revealed that residents' satisfaction was influenced by traffic problems and street cleanliness. Dahmann (1985) has shown that residents' satisfaction is inversely related to city size. Galster and Hester (1981) have found that certain groups (younger, those with many children) include lower levels of satisfaction in any context. These findings, of course, represent generalizations.

2 **Analyze discourse:** Look back at Activity 1 and at the discovery verbs and existence verbs you circled or underlined. Write the tense of each of these verbs in the margin. Draw an arrow between the verb and its tense.

3 **Practice the structure:** Complete each passage with the present perfect, simple past, or present tense of the verb in parentheses. Use the meaning of the verb (discovery or existence) and the context (showing current relevance/importance or not) to determine the correct tense. Be ready to explain your choice to a partner.

1. Previous research at Syracuse University _____has shown_____ that online searches
   (show)

   are not very successful. This depressing finding is consistent with recent studies at other universities.

2. Research studies _____ a number of common problems for users of
   (uncover)

   online catalogs. The major problems include failed searches, no matches, and navigational confusion.

3. Honey and Hall (1989) _____ no difference between groups who were
   (find)

   trained differently. But Honey and Hall (1990) conducted a further study that eliminated problems in the research design.

4. The method in this book is the one introduced by Bury (1935). This _____
   (consist of)

   writing down the structures. . . .

5. Researchers _____ that secondary school teachers think of examinations
   (find)

   in three different ways. For some, they are a constraint. Other teachers think they are a resource for motivating pupils. . . .

6. The 1980 census _____ marked differences by gender and region. . .
   (reveal)

   In 1983 a major reform program was launched.

7. All research projects _____ a hypothesis, since the research process is a
   (depend on)

   detailed test of the relationship between variables. What then is a hypothesis?

4 Practice writing: Use the notes in the box to write a paragraph about cigarette smoking in the United States. Use at least two discovery verbs in the present prefect to highlight results that continue to be relevant or important. Use at least one existence verb to describe a current state.

> • 1964 U.S. Surgeon General's study (and numerous later studies): cigarette smoking—serious health hazard with risks like lung cancer, heart disease, stroke, and birth defects.
> • 1971: TV ads for cigarettes—banned due to health risks
>   sales of cigarettes—banned to people under the age of 18
> • 1980s: U.S. Congress requirement—stronger warning labels on cigarette ads
> • 1988 U.S. Surgeon General's study: nicotine (an ingredient in cigarettes)—addictive
> • Now: health risks of cigarette smoking well known, smoking bans in public buildings in many cities, cigarette use still increasing with young people

The dangers of cigarette smoking are well researched; however, warnings by the Surgeon General of the United States have had mixed success in decreasing cigarette use in the United States. Many studies **have shown** that . . . _____

_____

_____

_____

_____

I didn't get a chance . . .
Meanings of *Get*

What have you learned from your grammar textbook?

The verb **get** has several uses. (**1**) It can mean "obtain or receive something." (**2**) It can mean "become." (**3**) It can show that a person causes something to happen. (**4**) It can be used for passive voice.

1. I **got a letter** from my friend.
2. I **got hot** in the sun.
3. I will **get my hair cut** tomorrow.
4. The boy **got caught** when he broke the window.

A) What does the corpus show?

Get is an extremely **common verb** in **conversation** because it has so many different uses and meanings. Here are **five common meanings** for *get* when it is used as a **main verb**:

Expression with *Get*	Meaning	Example
get + **noun phrase**	1. obtain or receive something	• I'm trying to figure out how we can *get* **some cash**.
get + **adjective**	2. become*	• It *got* **cold** at night. • I'm really sorry. I'm *getting* **confused**.
get home *get here / there* *get* + *to*-phrase	3. arrive at a place	• Did you just *get home*? • I don't know if he'll *get here* on time. • When you *get to* **Broad Street**, make a left.
get it	4. understand a story or joke	• I don't *get it*. [After hearing a story.]
get + **noun phrase** + **participle**	5. cause something to happen	• It took a little while to *get* **the car fixed**.

*"Become" is a common meaning for *getting* + **adjective**.

B)

Get + **noun phrase** often has a more idiomatic meaning than "obtain or receive." Here are **five common useful expressions** with *get* + noun that are **more idiomatic**:

Fixed Expression with *Get*	Meaning	Example
1. *get a chance*	have an opportunity	• I'm gonna chew gum until I *get a chance* to brush my teeth.
2. *get a job*	find work	• Why don't you *get a job* at one of the bike shops?
3. *get some sleep*	sleep	• Okay, *get some sleep* and take care! [To a sick friend.]
4. *get a hold of**	contact	• I might try one more time to *get a hold of* Kathy.
5. *get an idea of**	become familiar with	• Have lunch with us, so you can *get an idea of* our family.

* In some expressions, the preposition *of* follows the noun phrase.

C *Get* is also used in different **grammatical structures and idioms**:

Grammatical Structure / Idiom with *Get*	Example
1. auxiliary verb for **passive voice**	• Well, Hannah *got punished* the other day.
2. modal ***have got to*** (often pronounced *gotta*)	• Yeah, you *gotta* hear this.
3. ***have got*** (meaning *have* in American English)	• *I've got* a question for you.
4. **phrasal verbs***	• Did you *get up* in time to see the parade?
5. **idiomatic expressions**	• They *got rid of* everything.

*See Units 13–15 for more on phrasal verbs with *get*.

D **Be careful!** In **writing** and **formal speaking**, more formal and precise verbs and expressions are often used instead of *get*. For example, writers might use ***obtain, arrive,*** or ***have the opportunity***.

Activities

1 Notice in context: Read these conversations aloud with a partner. Then circle each *get* phrase.

1. *Max enters Paulo's office.*

PAULO: Morning, Max.

MAX: Morning. Oh, Paulo?

PAULO: Mmm hmmm?

MAX: Uh, I need to get a hold of Mr Sunyatta.

PAULO: Okay, so you want his phone number?

MAX: Yes. And here's the form for the project that Nicky is doing.

PAULO: If you get a chance, could you fill it out for me?

2. *Two university employees talk.*

MANA: I got a call from a student who wanted help contacting, um, that computer science professor. But I think they don't use their answering machines over in that department.

DIEGO: You gotta email them.

MANA: Yes, that's true.

2 Analyze discourse: Look back at Activity 1 and at the *get* phrases that you circled. Write the meaning of each phrase in the margin. Draw an arrow between the phrase and its meaning.

3 Practice the structure: Each of these excerpts from informational writing has a *get* phrase that is more appropriate for conversation. Circle each *get* phrase and write a more formal expression to replace it on the line below.

1. Men who were farmers in a training program were asked about the most suitable time of day to take a class. Afternoons were chosen by two-thirds. Their wives also chose afternoons: they could attend classes knowing they would get home in time for the children returning from school.

_____

(continued on next page)

2. Many employers seek to get a relatively cheap workforce, either by self-employment on special projects or by direct employment of workers who are part-time workers.

   _____

3. Computer owners who would like to control a baseball team themselves get a chance to play team manager with two new computer games endorsed by men who have been World Series winners.

   _____

4 **Practice conversation:** Two friends are talking about going to a movie together. They agree to ask another friend to join them. Complete their conversation using *get* phrases that have the meanings listed in the box. Then practice the conversation with a partner.

have an opportunity	obtain something	arrive at a place
contact	understand	

A: Did you **get a chance** to see that new martial arts movie?

B: Not yet. Want to go this Friday?

A: _____

B: _____

A: _____

B: _____

A: _____

B: _____

Did you have fun today?
Meanings of *Have* + Noun Phrase

What have you learned from your grammar textbook?

Have is an **irregular** verb (*have – has – had – had*). It can be used both as an **auxiliary verb** and as a **main verb**. The literal **meaning of *have*** when it is a **main verb** is "to own or possess something":

A: What kind of car *does* he *have*?
B: He *has* a jeep.

What does the corpus show?

A *Have* is an extremely **common verb** in both **conversation** and **writing** because it has many different meanings and uses. *Have* + **noun phrase** is a common structure. But its **literal meaning** "to own or possess something" **is rare**.

• I need to make sure I *have* **enough money** in my account.

B In **conversation**, several **nouns** are especially **common with *have***. These combinations express the following **idiomatic meanings**:

Meaning	Common Nouns with *Have* in Conversation			Example
1. eat/drink something	*dinner*	*lunch*	*a drink*	• I said we might *have dinner* with him.
2. enjoy something	*fun*	*a good time*		• I hope you *have fun* at your party.
3. experience difficulty	*trouble*	*a hard time*	*a problem*	• I *have trouble* going up and down stairs.
4. not be bothered by something	*no problem (with)*			• He *has no problem with* arithmetic.
5. create a family	*kids*	*children*	*a baby*	• They get married, then they *have kids*.
6. get an opportunity/ time to do something	*a chance* *time*	*the chance*		• We didn't *have a chance* to watch it.
7. be thinking about something	*an idea*	*no idea*	*a question*	• I *have no idea* who she is.

C In **writing**, a **different set of nouns** are **common with *have***. Most of these nouns occur with a specific **preposition** and have **special meanings**.

Common Nouns with *Have* in Writing		Preposition	Example
an effect *little effect* *no effect*	*an impact* *little influence* *no influence*	*on*	• Banning book bags at the school will *have little effect on* the drug problem.
the advantage *a range* *a wide variety*	*little evidence* *no evidence* *no knowledge*	*of*	• Elderly people may *have a range of* social connections.

(continued on next page)

Common Nouns with *Have* in Writing		Preposition	Example
the potential little sympathy	*implications*	*for*	• Objective measuring **has definite implications for** quality assurance.
an interest	*a role*	*in*	• The teacher **has a role in** encouraging the pupil to use the learning aid.

Other common nouns in writing **are followed by a *to*-clause**. The pattern is: ***have* + noun + *to*-clause**.

a duty to	*good reason to*	*a (the) right to*	*the ability to*	*the potential to*
a tendency to	*no reason to*	*no right to*	*the opportunity to*	*power to*

- Some people **have a tendency to** rationalize and justify their decisions.
- Kotler **had the opportunity to** quit smoking but chose to continue his habit.

Activities

1 **Notice in context:** Read the conversation and the sentences from academic writing. Circle each instance of the main verb ***have*** and underline the noun phrase that follows. If a preposition follows the noun, draw a square around it.

   1. **Conversation:** *About a friend who had a baby.*

     BARBARA: Have you talked to Angie lately?

     JENNIFER: We need to talk but she hasn't had time. And, um, anyway, I didn't know Angie had a baby. See, goes to show how much I know.*

     BARBARA: You didn't know about that already? I had no idea that you didn't know that!

   2. **Academic writing:** *About an education course.*

     a. When it is actualized through classroom activity, it can have an effect on learning.

     b. Quasi-experiments have the advantage of being practical when conditions prevent true experimentation.

     c. As participants in the learning/teaching operation, pupils have a role in the evaluation process, working together to monitor the effects of classroom activity.

––––––––––––––––––

   * ***goes to show how much I know*** is an idiom that means "That shows that I don't know very much."

2 **Practice conversation:** Read the conversation. Change each boldfaced phrase to a ***have* + noun phrase** to make the conversation sound more natural. Write this new expression on the line next to the phrase. Then practice the new conversation with two partners.

Brian and Robert are inviting Doug to go on a hike to a mountain resort.

     BRIAN: Yeah, you know, we go and **eat a meal** up there.   <u>have lunch</u>
                 It's kind of a—not a hard hike, but it takes about half an hour.

     DOUG: Let's see. I don't know if I will **be free** to go.   ––––––––––––––––––

ROBERT: Yeah. We haven't gone in awhile because it's so hot up in the mountains. Have you ever **been able** to do it?

            _____

DOUG: No, but I **want to ask something**. What would you say the temperature is up there?

            _____

ROBERT: Oh, by our house it's about seventy. If you want to come, come. If you don't, we won't **feel upset about that**.

            _____

DOUG: Good. Well, I just want to **enjoy myself**.

            _____

BRIAN: That's good.

3 **Practice writing:** Describe your own experience as a language learner. Use **_have_ + noun phrase** to write six statements.

EXAMPLE

Students should **have the opportunity to** practice new words.
Playing football **has little influence on** learning a language.

1. _____

2. _____

3. _____

4. _____

5. _____

6. _____

It really made a difference . . .
Meanings of *Make* + Noun Phrase

What have you learned from your grammar textbook?

Make is an **irregular verb** (*make – made – made*). (**1**) It means "to produce or create something." (**2**) It can also show that a person causes something to be done.

1. The boy *made* a paper airplane.

2. The doctor *made* my back better.

What does the corpus show?

A *Make* is an extremely **common verb** in both **conversation** and **writing** because it has many different meanings and uses. *Make* + **noun phrase** is a common structure. The literal meaning is "to produce something," but this **literal meaning is not common**.

- I was going to *make* **a gingerbread house** this year.

B In **conversation**, several **nouns** are especially **common with** *make*. These combinations express the following **idiomatic meanings**:

Meaning	Common Nouns with *Make* in Conversation		Example
1. perform an action	*the bed* *a phone call*		• Can I *make a phone call*, please?
2. produce talk and sounds	*a joke* *a speech*	*(a) noise* *(a) sound*	• It *makes a little squeaky noise* every time I bend it.
3. plan or decide to do something	*an appointment* *arrangements to* *a decision to*	*a deal* *plans to*	• Well, have you *made plans to* see Carol again?
4. earn money	*a living* *money*	*a profit*	• They *made a lot of money* in that business.
5. have an effect	*a difference*		• I worked out every day. It really *made a difference*.
6. try hard	*an effort*		• You should *make an effort* to meet with those kids.
7. do something wrong	*a mistake*		• I *made a mistake* with this word.
8. be reasonable	*sense* *no sense*		• No other conclusion *makes sense*.
9. tease someone	*fun of*		• Yeah, at work they *make fun of* me.
10. have time free for a person/ activity	*time for*		• I will *make time for* you before the end of the week.

C In writing, the **nouns used with** *make* are often **more abstract** but usually express **idiomatic meanings:**

Meaning	Common Nouns with *Make* in Writing		Example
1. describe a mental activity	*assumptions* *comparisons* *judgments*	*choices* *decisions*	• In the current absence of information, one can only *make assumptions* based on impressions . . .
2. describe what will (or should) happen in the future	*predictions* *recommendations*		• The budget committees will *make recommendations* for spending levels.
3. be reasonable	*sense* *no sense*		• It therefore *makes sense* to analyze urban morphology in an historical context.
4. use something	*use of*		• Learners will *make use of* translation because the learning process requires them to do so.
5. refer to other information	*reference to*		• Most other authors *make reference to* this article by Duncan.

Activities

1 Notice in context: Read these passages. Notice that the first one and the last two reproduce direct speech or conversation. Underline the examples of *make* + **noun phrase**.

1. *From a book giving advice to mountain climbers.*

   "We also feel a high carbohydrate diet can make a difference. Mountain climber studies show that on a carbohydrate diet, they feel better rather than when on a fatty diet," he said. The study hopes to eventually provide information so people can make informed decisions about whether to go to high altitudes and how to prepare for such trips.

2. *From a textbook about the decision process.*

   All decisions involve prediction of the likely consequences of actions. To make a prediction, the decision-maker must have a model of the environment which is being influenced.

3. *From a woman's letter from a war zone.*

   "It doesn't make any sense how we have to scurry to the cold, damp bomb shelters whenever there is a raid, now almost every night," she wrote. "I am so weary of it all. I would rather get a good night's sleep and be bombed in bed."

4. *From an article giving advice to parents.*

   "You can see the difference in the kids involved," Kelly said. "When you make time for your kids, it makes them feel special. So if they feel they're important, they try a little harder."

2 **Analyze discourse:** Each example below has a phrase in bold. Match it with a phrase from the box that has the same meaning. Write the letter of your choice on the line next to the example.

> **a.** *make a decision*   **c.** *makes sense*   **e.** *make use of*
> **b.** *make plans*   **d.** *make an effort*   **f.** *make a difference*

_a_ **1.** Some parents take on debt to pay for high-quality child care. Pat Ward and her husband, parents of two, borrowed money from her parents to pay for an experienced caregiver for her first child and a neighbor's child in New York City. "We had to **decide** about our priorities," says Ms. Ward.

_____ **2.** Davis's breakthrough came in the early 1920s, when he began to use imagery taken from advertising. The artist's decision to **use** the imagery of consumerism resulted in some of his most original art works, such as his celebrated images incorporating cigarette packages.

_____ **3.** From a newspaper story about Unequal Educational Opportunities: "Money does **have an effect**," education officials told a House of Representatives committee Wednesday as disagreements erupted over public school finances.

Two friends talk about a meeting:

_____ **4.** LIN: Well, I'll call you tomorrow to **plan what we'll do**.

_____ **5.** MAI: OK. Should I **try hard** to borrow a car Wednesday?

_____ **6.** LIN: That **sounds reasonable**. That way you can drop me off at work.

3 **Practice conversation:** Complete the following conversation. Use four phrases with *make* from Section B. Make sure your conversation makes sense! When you are finished, practice your conversation with a partner.

A: Can I **make a call** on your cell phone?

B: Sure, but be careful. If you **make a mistake,** _____

A: _____

B: _____

A: _____

B: _____

4 **Practice writing:** Write a paragraph that *makes* some *comparisons* between riding a bicycle and using a car or bus. For example, does driving *make sense* if air pollution is a problem? Should people *make use of* a bicycle only for fun? What *recommendations* can you *make* for the best use of cars and bicycles? Use at least five *make* + *noun phrases* that are common in writing.

There are several advantages to using a bicycle instead of a car or bus. First, . . .

_____

_____

_____

_____

_____

_____

Let's take a look at it
Meanings of *Take* + Noun Phrase

What have you already learned from your grammar textbook?

Take is an **irregular verb** (*take – took – taken*). The literal **meaning of *take*** is "to move or carry something from one place to another":

- I ***took*** the cake out of the oven.

What does the corpus show?

A *Take* is an extremely **common verb** in both conversation and writing because it has many different meanings and uses. *Take* + **noun phrase** is a common structure. But its **literal meaning** "to move or carry something from one place of the other" **is rare**.

- You should ***take*** the garage door opener so you can get in.

B In conversation, several **nouns** are especially **common with *take***. These combinations express many different **idiomatic meanings**:

Meaning	Common Nouns with *Take* in Conversation			Example
1. use a camera	*a photo*	*a picture*		• She ***took a picture*** of Sara eating lobster.
2. get washed	*a bath*	*a shower*		• I'm going to ***take a bath***.
3. sleep or rest	*a nap*	*a break*	*it easy*	• I'm going to go ***take a break***.
4. happen or occur	*place*			• Is that where the story ***took place***?
5. spend enough time for a task	*a minute*	*time*		• This will only ***take a minute***.
6. complete a school task	*classes*	*a course*	*a test*	• I had to ***take a test*** today.
7. write something	*a message*	*notes*		• Would you like me to ***take a message***?
8. use a car or vehicle	*a car*	*the bus*	*a ride*	• I ***took the bus*** from Los Angeles.
9. go in a different direction	*a right*	*a left (turn)*		• ***Take a left*** on Reynolds Avenue.
10. look at something	*a look at**			• Is it OK if I ***take a look at*** those pictures?
11. make sure that some task is done properly	*care of** *charge of** *responsibility for**			• Don't worry about it – she already ***took care of*** everything.

*In some expressions a preposition like ***at***, ***of***, or ***for*** follows the noun phrase.

C In writing, other **nouns** are **common with** *take*. These nouns often occur with a specific **preposition** and have **special meanings**:

Meaning	Common Nouns with *Take* in Writing	Example
1. begin work on a task	*action* *the lead in* *the initiative* *steps to*	• The registered nurses in the ward team ***take the lead in*** this process.
2. argue for a point of view	*the position that* *the view that*	• Some experts ***take the view that*** the original judgment was false.
3. consider something	*account of* *into account*	• The researcher needs to ***take account of*** these factors.
4. participate	*part in*	• 176 patients ***took part in*** the experiment.
5. exploit	*advantage of*	• Queretaro ***takes advantage of*** its prime location.
6. be regarded as more important	*precedence over*	• The needs of the patient ***take precedence over*** the needs of the learner.
7. describing how something is realized	*the form of* *the shape of*	• Unit provision usually ***takes the form of*** providing a home base in a separate room.

Activities

1 **Notice in context:** Read the conversation and the sentences from academic writing. Circle each instance of *take* and underline the noun phrase that follows. If there is a preposition, underline it too.

1. **Conversation:** *In an office.*

   RECEPTIONIST: (*on the phone*) Um, no he's not. May I take a message? . . . Okay, how do you spell your name? . . . Okay. Sure. Bye bye.

   VISITOR: Hi. I'm here to see Mary.

   RECEPTIONIST: Okay, Mary's office, I don't even know if she's here, but go down through the hall and then take a left, and it's the second door on the right.

   VISITOR: Thank you.

2. **Academic writing:** *About long-term medical care for children.*

   a. The worker was committed to the idea that treatment of a medical or disabling condition should not take precedence over the child's social, emotional, and cultural needs.

   b. Many children will require day-to-day support as well as encouragement that takes into account both their social backgrounds and their specific medical condition.

   c. It is a good practice to pay attention to the child's attitude during treatment to try to pinpoint the cause of any negative feelings and to take steps to remedy the situation.

2 **Practice conversation:** You and a friend are training to become lifeguards at a local pool. Your friend has been on vacation, and you need to tell him what he has missed. Use **take + noun phrase** to make these lines sound more like informal conversation. When you are finished, say these more informal lines to a partner.

1. Maria completed a course on first aid. Maria **took a course** on first aid.
2. The course was only two days long. _____
3. We need to learn how to fix problems. _____
4. I examined our summer training schedule. _____
5. Our next session will be held across town. _____
6. We can use the bus to get there. _____

3 **Practice writing:** Summarize the following situations using **take + noun phrase**. Make sure you use the correct form of the verb.

1. Juan wants to spend more time at home with his family than at his job, because family is what is most important to him.

   Summary: Juan's family _____ over his job.

2. Georgia got a head start and prepared the materials she and her group would need to start on their new physics project.

   Summary: Georgia _____ on the physics project.

3. The committee voted to require all students to wear uniforms last November, but the new policy did not consider the cost of uniforms.

   Summary: The new policy did not _____ the cost of uniforms.

4. Lauren argued that because she had worked hard for the company for the past year, she deserved a pay raise.

   Summary: Lauren _____ that she deserved a raise.

I felt good about it
Linking Verbs

What have you learned from your grammar textbook?

Linking verbs can be followed by an **adjective**. The adjective describes the subject of the sentence. Linking verbs can describe (**1**) a **state** of existence, or (**2**) a **change** to a new state:

  1. He *seems* happy.   **2.** The weather *became* worse.

What does the corpus show?

A The linking verb *be* is common in both conversation and writing. But otherwise, some linking verbs are preferred in conversation; others in writing. Here is a list of the **most common linking verbs** used either in conversation or in writing:

	Linking Verb	Example
1. conversation	*feel* *get** *go* *look*	• I *feel* stupid every time I go over there. • Maybe I should go in and *get* ready. • There was a disease and all the potatoes *went* bad. • Lila *looks* good.
2. writing	*become* *remain* *seem*	• It then *became* necessary to discover the cause of the change. • Energy costs have risen since the early 1970s, but fertilizer use *remains* highly cost effective. • The second part *seems* more vulnerable than the first.

* See Unit 4 about the meanings of *get*.

B Most linking verbs describe **specific meanings**, and as a result they occur with a **particular set of adjectives**:

Verb	Describes	Following Adjectives			Example
feel	physical sensations	*better* *cold*	*good* *sick*	*tired* *uncomfortable*	• My hands *feel cold*.
	mental sensations	*ashamed* *bad*	*guilty* *sure*	*uneasy*	• I *feel bad* for her.
get	a change to a negative state	*angry* *bored* *cold* *lost*	*mad* *sick* *tired*	*upset* *wet* *worse*	• He *got mad* when I told him.
go	a change to a negative state	*bad* *crazy*	*deaf* *limp*	*mad* *wrong*	• But something *went wrong*, because they weren't ready.
look	positive feelings about physical appearance	*good* *happy*	*lovely* *nice*		• Your hair *looks nice*.
	negative feelings about physical appearance	*awful* *pale*	*sad* *small*	*terrible* *tired*	• There's some meat in there that *looks* really *awful*.

Verb	Describes	Following Adjectives			Example
become	a change in understanding or importance	*apparent* *clear*	*difficult* *evident*	*familiar* *important*	• The importance of this idea will *become apparent* later.
remain	an absence of change	*closed* *constant*	*intact* *uncertain*	*unchanged* *unknown*	• The speed of the flow *remains constant*.
seem	likelihood	*clear* *likely*	*obvious* *possible*	*reasonable* *unlikely*	• It *seems likely* new systems will be easier to write.

Activities

1 Notice in context: Read the conversation and the paragraph from an academic text. Circle the linking verbs, except *be*.

1. **Conversation:** *About a friend who is sick.*

   DANA: I saw Janelle the other day. She got extremely sick. I mean she stays in bed all the time. She should go to the hospital.

   LORI: Really? I think she looks good. I saw her yesterday. Was she pretending when I saw her?

   DANA: Yeah, she's very good at pretending. She's actually really sick right now.

2. **Academic writing:** *About school exams.*

   According to the traditional pattern of school examinations, there has been a separation of the sciences: biology, chemistry, and physics. The new plan, on the other hand, is more concerned with problem-solving across all the sciences. The final phase of academic school examinations, which differs from vocational examinations, seems likely to remain unchanged for the foreseeable future.

2 Analyze discourse: Answer the following questions. Follow the instructions.

1. What is the subject of each of the linking verbs you circled in the conversation and paragraph above? Underline each subject.

2. What adjective is connected to each subject by the linking verb? Double underline each adjective.

3 Practice conversation: Read each situation and follow the instructions.

1. Robert and Daniel are at home after picking up their sister Lauren from the airport after her flight was cancelled. Complete their conversation with *feel, get, go,* and *look*. Each verb will be used once. When you are finished, practice the conversation with two partners.

   ROBERT: Lauren, are you cold in here? Let's turn the thermostat up a little bit. I just don't want us to _____ sick.

   DANIEL: What did you think when you found out that your flight was cancelled?

   LAUREN: Oh, for some reason, I was hardly surprised. I guess I was just expecting something to _____ wrong.

   DANIEL: Uh huh. Well, you _____ tired.

   LAUREN: Yeah, I _____ all right. I just don't want to go back to the airport tomorrow.

(continued on next page)

2. With a partner go to a public area, like an airport or a park, and observe the people there. Choose a couple of people. Describe their behavior to your partner and make comments about how they might be feeling, using *feel, get, go,* and *look*.

EXAMPLE

[At a library] That girl with her head on the table **looks** really tired.

4 **Practice writing:** Look at the pictures. Write a paragraph related to each picture. Use **become, remain,** and **seem** with common adjectives.

1.
Although several computers burst into flames, the office workers tried to **remain** . . .

_____

_____

_____

2.
The cost of education **seems** . . .

_____

_____

_____

Tell me that story
Verbs with Two Objects

What have you learned from your grammar textbook?

Many verbs can occur with two objects. The **direct object (DO)** identifies the thing influenced by the action of the verb, while the **indirect object (IO)** identifies the person who received the action. The indirect object can come first or second.

When the **indirect object comes first**, this is the grammatical pattern: **V + IO + DO.**

               V   IO   DO
* Maybe he *gave* **you** *the wrong book.*

When the **indirect object comes second**, we use the preposition *to* or *for*: **V + DO + *to/for* + IO.**

               V   DO   Pp   IO
* I'm going to *send* *fifty dollars* **to my cousin.**

What does the corpus show?

A   Many of **the most common verbs** in English can occur **with two objects**.

ask	*give*	*sell*	*take*
bring	*make*	*send*	*tell*
buy	*offer*	*show*	
get	*promise*		

* Would you *bring* **me** *a cup of coffee?*
* He *gave* **her** *a letter.*
* I could *show* **him** *my map.*

* I *bought* *a dress* **for you.**
* She *sold* *the house* **to Wally.**

B   Several of these verbs usually occur **with special grammatical patterns**.

Verb	Grammatical Pattern	Examples
show *tell* *ask*	**V + IO + clause/infinitive phrase DO** (with indirect object; direct object = dependent clause or infinitive phrase)	• I'll *show* **him** *how everything works.* • I *told* **her** *that I was going on a trip.* • I'm gonna *ask* **Mom** *to get me the wallet.*
promise	**V + clause/infinitive phrase DO** (no indirect object; direct object = dependent clause or infinitive phrase)	• We can't *promise* *that we can solve the problems.* • They *promised* *to write.*
bring	**V + noun phrase DO + adverbial** (no indirect object; direct object = noun phrase; usually occurs with an adverbial)	• I *brought* *that book* **home.**

C The **order of the two objects** is usually determined by the length of each object. The **longer object goes last.**

	Description of Use	Examples
1. **direct object is longer** than indirect object	• direct object is a noun phrase or a clause • indirect object is usually a very short noun phrase or a pronoun	• That gives **employees** *the skills they need.* • I told **my dad** *that my brakes didn't work very well.* • Her parents just bought **her** *a new half sized violin.*
2. **indirect object is longer** than direct object	• indirect object is a noun phrase used with **to** or **for** • direct object is usually a pronoun	• She gave *it* **to her best friend.** • He bought *them* **for his daughter.**

Be careful! If **both objects are pronouns,** the order is: **V + DO + *to/for* + IO.**

• Give *that* **to me.**

Activities

1 **Notice in context:** Read the conversation. Some of the boldfaced verbs have one object, and some have two objects. Underline the direct object and circle the indirect object, if there is one.

Discussing a used car that stopped working.

BILL: They **sold** me their Volkswagen van and I'm not driving it right now because it's not running well. They **told** me they'd stop by sometime tonight and look at it.

JANET: Hmm, why did you buy it if it's not working?

BILL: Well, they **brought** it over here and they said it's running real good.

JANET: Hmm. Maybe somebody had been working on it. Um, so you already paid for it?

BILL: Most of it. Uh, I **promised** to pay more, but I don't know . . .

JANET: Yeah, you should **ask** them what they think about it now that it's not running.

2 **Analyze and edit:** These sentences were written by English-language learners. For each boldfaced verb, find the object(s) and decide if they are in the correct order. If the sentence is correct, write *C* on the line. If it is incorrect, correct it. Remember, some direct objects may be entire clauses, and not all sentences have indirect objects.

the children

_____ **1.** The parents have to **show** ∧ that it is important to solve problems together in the family to the children.

_____ **2.** I am going to **make** you a list of things to bring on vacation.

_____ **3.** Now if you have some time, I will **tell** where the apartment is to you.

_____ **4.** I'll **send** you my address, and I **promise** you to do well and be good.

_____ **5.** My friends might **bring** some gifts and cards to me.

_____ **6.** I **asked** if it's true that he never watched television to the prisoner.

3 **Practice the structure:** Each sentence contains both a direct and an indirect object (in parentheses), but they may be out of order. Rewrite the sentence on the line. Make sure the objects are in the correct order.

1. She showed (how to boil the meat / them).
   <u>She showed **them how to boil the meat.**</u>

2. Arnold picks apples and brings (them / to his family).
   _____

3. She told (that she was afraid of driving in the snow / him).
   _____

4. I bought (for him / it).
   _____

5. I asked (if this was the correct address / them).
   _____

4 **Practice conversation:** Get to know a classmate better. Ask each other questions about family, school, leisure activities, etc. Use the verb in parentheses in each question and answer. Include both a direct and an indirect object in each answer (unless the verb has a special grammatical structure without one). After you talk, write down your questions and answers.

(give)   **A:** <u>What do you **give your mother** for her birthday?</u>

          B: <u>Usually I **give her flowers**.</u>

(show)   **A:** _____

          B: _____

(bring)   **A:** _____

          B: _____

(send)   **A:** _____

          B: _____

(tell)   **A:** _____

          B: _____

(ask)   **A:** _____

          B: _____

Reports suggest that . . .
Action Verbs with Inanimate Subjects

Academic Writing

What have you learned from your grammar textbook?

With transitive verbs in active voice, the subject is usually the actor who performed the action. **Transitive verbs** have a **direct object (DO)**. **Intransitive action verbs** also usually have a subject who performed the activity, but there is **no direct object**.

S   V   DO
TRANSITIVE: **The boy** *kicked* the ball.

S   V
INTRANSITIVE: **The girl** *worked* for five hours.

A What does the corpus show?

In academic writing, certain action verbs often have **inanimate subjects**. In real life, these subjects cannot perform an action, but they are used like human actors. **Three major types** of inanimate subjects are very common:

Type of Subject	Description of Use	Examples
1. texts	Ideas seem to come from the text rather than the writer.	• **Reports** *suggest* that in many subject areas, textbooks and materials are not available. • **This article** *explains* how decisions were made to design a test.
2. subject areas, abstract ideas, actions or processes	We assume that people are creating or using the abstract ideas and subjects.	• **New fields of study** *have developed* their own methodologies. • **Important and complex decisions** *take* time.
3. research work	Research studies, or results or evidence from research are used as subjects.	• **Other studies** *have found* that the power of managers is limited. • **More conclusive evidence** *comes* from other experiments.

B Inanimate subjects have a **variety of functions**. More than one function can occur at the same time.

1. Inanimate subjects give more **emphasis to the inanimate thing** than to a human actor.
2. Sometimes the **human actor is not known**, not important, or is "people" in general.
3. Some writers think the **ideas sound more objective** when the human actor is not named.
4. Sometimes an **abstract concept is the topic** of the discourse.

These functions are related to the use of **passive voice in research writing** (*see Unit 16*).

C When **transitive verbs** are used with **abstract, inanimate subjects**, they also often have **direct objects that are abstract**.

Type of Direct Object	Examples
1. abstract noun phrase	• A review of publications *shows* diverse and even contradictory results. • Spatial contexts *provide* crucial information about the behavior of ancient people.
2. clause expressing an abstract idea	• This study *indicates* that proficiency in language is important. • The review of the literature *has demonstrated* that use of the verb be in Spanish varies.

D **Frequency information.** Many different action verbs occur with inanimate subjects in academic writing. Here is a list of the **most common action verbs that have inanimate subjects:**

come	find	indicate	need	show	take
explain	give	lead	provide	suggest	

- The "Adjusted Trial Balance" columns *give* the adjusted account balances.
- Results *indicated* that all participants preferred to work for companies with merit-based pay systems.
- Further cooling *leads* to condensation.
- The slopes of the lines in the graphs *show* how sensitive the project's NPV is to changes in each of the inputs.

Activities

1 **Notice in context:** Read these excerpts from different academic texts. Underline each inanimate subject that has an action verb with it. Circle the action verb. Be careful! Some of the verbs are in the list of most common action verbs, but others are not.

1. *A study about taking multiple choice tests.*

This study investigates whether answer-changing on multiple choice tests is beneficial. An exam was given to 286 students. Findings suggest that we should encourage students to change their answers after they look at them and find better answers.

2. *Advice for studying language learning.*

An investigation of language acquisition requires methods that include native speakers in the design. These methods must also provide a framework for comparing native speakers and learners.

3. *Advice for encouraging new ideas in teaching.*

Most good ideas come from working towards a goal. For example, suppose you are trying to introduce teachers of English to the computer and show them its value as an aid to their teaching.

4. *A textbook description of accounting practices.*

Businesses need periodic reports on their progress. Accountants slice time into small segments and prepare financial statements for specific periods. Until a business sells all its assets for cash and pays all its liabilities, the amounts reported in its financial statements must be regarded as estimates.

2 **Analyze discourse:** Look back at Activity 1 and at the inanimate subjects you underlined. Write each one below. Then next to it, write its function(s). Use the information in Section B if you need help recognizing the functions.

1. _____

_____

2. _____

_____

3. _____

_____

4. _____

_____

3 **Practice writing:** Write these scrambled sentences in correct word order. Each one contains an inanimate subject. The first word in each sentence is capitalized. Circle the direct object and note if it has an abstract meaning.

1. indicated / Reports on care for the elderly / that the quality was generally poor

   _____

2. from the desire / come / Some actions which benefit others / to help that particular person

   _____

3. a better insulated material / The technique of combining plastic and plywood / for walls / produces

   _____

4. should be restrictive / explains / why the conditions for compensation / The second principle

   _____

5. that reaction occurs by a polar mechanism / These facts / to the conclusion / lead

   _____

4 **Practice writing:** Imagine that you have read a study on a topic that interests you. Write a paragraph to summarize that study, using "facts" that you invent. Use at least three action verbs with inanimate subjects.

EXAMPLE

The **study found** that ice cream gives pleasure to many people, but it also has a lot of fat. Ice cream provides calories without nutrition. **This fact suggests** that ice cream should have a small place in your diet since **bad diet decisions lead** to health problems.

_____

_____

_____

_____

I might go to Japan
Possibility Modals

What have you learned from your grammar textbook?

Modals show a speaker's attitude toward what he or she is saying. Different modals express different meanings, such as whether something is possible or necessary. An individual modal can also express **different meanings depending on context**. For example, *can* has the following meanings and functions:

Meaning	Function	Example
be able to be possible be allowed to	describing an **ability** indicating a **possibility** asking **permission**	• I *can* see the Statue of Liberty from my house. • Knowledge of local culture *can* be important. • *Can* I turn the radio on?

What does the corpus show?

A The modals *can, could, might, may* all express the meaning that something is **possible**. But some of these modals are also used to express **ability,** ask **permission,** or make a **request**. Here are some of their **most common uses** in conversation and writing.

Modal	Function	Conversation or Writing?	Examples
can	1. **ability:** describing what someone is able to do	• the most common meaning • common in both conversation and writing	• I *can* cross my eyes. • The preparation *can* be carried out in a short period.
	2. **ability and possibility:** describing what someone is able to do *and* whether something is possible	• common in both conversation and writing	• I think it *can* be explained. • Gas and coal *can* displace oil in utility boilers.
	3. **permission or request:** asking permission or requesting something	• only in conversation	• *Can* I take off my jacket? [permission] • *Can* I have some more juice? [request]
could	1. **possibility:** indicating whether something is possible	• the most common meaning • less common than *can* • common in both conversation and writing	• That *could* be a problem. • The two processes *could* well be independent.
	2. **ability:** describing what someone is able to do	• only in conversation	• He *could* draw so well. • I knew she *could* find a job.
	3. **request:** requesting something	• only in conversation • more polite than *can*	• *Could* you do that one more time?
might	**possibility:** only used to show whether something is possible	• **not common** in conversation or writing	• I *might* do that. • This result *might* be compatible with a decrease in density.
may	**possibility:** showing whether something is possible	• common only in writing	• Female moths *may* exhibit movements between woodlands.

B Be careful! In **conversation**, *may* is **rarely** used to ask permission. Most people **use *can* or *could* to ask permission**. *Could* is more polite than *can*.

• *Can* I leave this here somewhere?   • *Could* I leave this here somewhere?

Activities

1 Notice in context: Read the conversation and the paragraph from an academic text. Circle the possibility modals in both.

1. **Conversation:** *Two friends looking for something to eat.*

   JANE: What else do you have in the kitchen? Can I just help myself?

   ANN: Sure. There's applesauce, grapes, and, well, that might be it.

   JANE: Okay. We could go out to a restaurant, you know, and get something to eat.

2. **Academic writing:** *About the potential benefits of computers in the classroom.*

   The speed of information processing of computers allows for thousands, even millions, of calculations each second. Computer programs can involve much more elaborate calculations than the teacher or the students can possibly complete in a class. The program may also simply do normal calculations for the teacher, thus freeing his attention for other matters in the classroom.

2 Analyze discourse: Look back at Activity 1 and at the modals you circled. Write the function (***ability, possibility, permission,*** or ***request***) of each one in the margin. Draw an arrow between the modal and its function. Remember, some modals can have multiple functions.

3 Practice conversation: Read the conversation. Then invent lines to complete it. Include a modal in each line. When you are finished, practice the conversation with a partner.

Jonathan and Danielle are in their car trying to follow directions on a map.

   JONATHAN: Which way do we go here?

   DANIELLE: Well, looking at the map, we have two choices: we <u>can</u> take a right here and then take the highway or _____.

   JONATHAN: Hold on, that doesn't make sense. _____.

   DANIELLE: Sure, here it is. You can try to figure it out.

   JONATHAN: This doesn't seem right. _____.

   DANIELLE: No, this isn't the wrong map. Wait, let me look at it.

   JONATHAN: Here is a gas station. _____.

   DANIELLE: OK, I'll ask for directions, but I'm sure this is the right map.

4 Practice writing: Read the paragraph about a boy who is having trouble learning to read. Then write five possible reasons why Stephen still cannot read. After each one, suggest a possible way of solving the problem. Use the possibility modals ***can, could, might,*** and ***may*** in your responses.

Stephen is in the first grade, and he is the only student in his class who still cannot read simple words. His teacher has observed the following things: Stephen avoids bright lights; he cannot copy letters or pictures from the blackboard; he has no books to read at home; he is younger than most of the other students in his class; he has no sisters or brothers; and he is clumsy and does not like to take part in physical activities.

EXAMPLE

REASON: Stephen **may** not have the same opportunities as the other students to read at home.
SUGGESTION: Perhaps, Stephen **could** practice with his parents at home.

1. _____
   _____

2. _____
   _____

3. _____
   _____

4. _____
   _____

5. _____
   _____

A compromise must be reached
Necessity Modals

What have you learned from your grammar textbook?

There are several **modals and phrasal modals** that express **necessity** or **certainty** meanings: *must, have to, have got to, should, ought to, had better*. Some of these modals can express **different meanings in different contexts**. For example, *must* can:

   1. describe a personal **obligation** (necessity meaning): • You *must* go to the party.
   2. refer to a logical **conclusion** (certainty meaning): • You *must* have been starving on that diet.

What does the corpus show?

A Some of these modals are preferred in conversation; others in writing. Each individual modal has different uses. Here are some of the **most common uses** in conversation and writing.

Modal	Function	Conversation or Writing?	Examples
must	1. **obligation:** describing what needs to be done	• relatively common in writing (often with a passive verb)	• The trade-offs faced by farmers *must* be carefully **considered**.
	2. **conclusions:** stating a logical conclusion	• relatively common in both conversation and writing (often with a verb in a perfect tense)	• He didn't know? Oh, so Mark *must* not **have told** him. • This climatic change *must* have **had** a significant impact on the habitat.
have to	**obligation:** expressing strong personal obligation	• very common in conversation	A: Why were you late? B: I *had to* close the building.
have got to (gotta*) *had better* (better**)	1. **obligation:** expressing personal obligations	• relatively common in conversation	• I've *got to* leave. • I'd *better* go.
	2. **advice:** making a recommendation	• relatively common in conversation	• You *gotta* get a sewing machine. • You *better* get going.
should	**advice:** asking for advice or recommending an action or procedure	• relatively common in conversation and writing (often with a passive verb)	• *Should* I try for it? • I think you *should* give this to Stephen. • Traps *should* be placed in locations of high moth density.

* *gotta:* Note that *have* in *have got to* is often dropped; *got to* is pronounced [gotta] in conversation.
****better:** Note that *had* in *had better* is often dropped.

B **Be careful!** In conversation, *must* is usually **NOT** used for **obligation** or to **give advice**. Use *have to* or *got to* instead. In academic writing, the modals *have to, have got to, had better,* and *ought to* are usually **NOT** used. Use *must* and *should* instead.

Activities

1 Notice in context: Read the sentences and circle the modals.

1. I remember my first car accident. It was right after I got my license, and I must have been sixteen. My dad was in the car with me and I backed into the car across the street.

2. In group counseling, comfortable seating should be used and chairs set out in a circle so that everyone can see each other. This is important for promoting trust and confidence in the group.

3. In the hospital's activity rooms, special care must be taken to ensure that the environment is safe for the patient to move around in.

4. I went hiking with people from work last week, and they were all talking about their relationships. So I thought, wow, I had better stay away from that. I haven't exactly been lucky with relationships.

2 Analyze discourse: Look back at the sentences in Activity 1. Decide whether each one is an example of conversation or academic writing. Base your decision on the choice of modal and its function. Compare your answers with a partner's.

1. Conversation ☐   Academic writing ☐
2. Conversation ☐   Academic writing ☐
3. Conversation ☐   Academic writing ☐
4. Conversation ☐   Academic writing ☐

3 Practice the structure: Which modal(s) would be a common choice to complete the sentences? Some sentences are examples of conversation, others of academic writing. There may be more than one answer.

1. **Conversation:**

   a. You're right. It's getting late. Yeah, you _____*better / should*_____ get going.

   b. I kept calling the wrong number. Well I guess I _____ have written it down wrong.

   c. See, I _____ take the test to drive here, because they won't accept my New York driver's license.

2. **Academic writing:**

   a. The first page of a scientific study _____ include the title of the study and the author's full name, along with the date of the final draft.

   b. The goals and objectives for a successful library education program _____ be based on a consideration of the needs of students.

4 Practice conversation: Offer advice to a classmate who wants to do the following things. Write three sentences for each of the student's goals. After you write your sentences, say them to a partner, practicing typical pronunciation (such as "you gotta" for "you have got to").

1. Improve writing skills in English.

   You **should** find a penpal.
   _____
   _____

(continued on next page)

2. Speak English more fluently.

You've **got to** practice often.

3. Comprehend academic lectures in English.

5 **Practice writing:** Your city council plans to destroy your neighborhood park in order to build an office building. You and your friends want to save the park. Use necessity modals to **(1)** recommend actions and **(2)** assign activities to people in the neighborhood to save the park.

1. _More community events **should** be scheduled to take place in the park._

2. _Someone **must** call the mayor's office._

Come on!
Phrasal Verbs

What have you learned from your grammar textbook?

Phrasal verbs consist of **two words: verb + particle** that together have a **special meaning**. They can be **transitive** (with an object) or **intransitive** (no object). They are most common in informal speech.

	V Pt O		V Pt
TRANSITIVE:	Please **turn out** the light.	INTRANSITIVE:	What time do you **get up** in the morning?

What does the corpus show?

A **Intransitive phrasal verbs** that refer to **activities** are very **common** in conversation and fiction writing, but rare in academic writing. They have two common uses:

Common Use of Intransitive Phrasal Verb	Example
1. commands, suggestions, or requests	• The lieutenant took a look at the person on the bench. "**Get up**," he said.
2. describing people's actions	• They **came over*** once for a barbeque.

***came over** = came to our house

B The single **most common** phrasal verb in conversation is intransitive **come on**. It has three typical uses:

Common Use of *Come on*	Example
1. exclamation or encouragement for someone to do something	• **Come on**, I'll teach you how to ski.
2. encouragement to get someone to move or leave	• **Come on**, let's get going.
3. meaning "to start" or "to be activated"	• Oh, that movie **came on** at five thirty.

C Surprisingly, many **transitive phrasal verbs** are common in both informal speech and formal writing. A few transitive phrasal verbs are even **more common in** academic writing than in conversation or fiction (*see Section E on next page*). These phrasal verbs usually sound more formal and precise than their one-word verb alternatives. Compare the following:

- We have **carried out** some laboratory research . . . → We have **done** some laboratory research . . .
- Pocock and Hudson (1978) **point out** that . . . → Pocock and Hudson (1978) **say** that . . .

D **Frequency information.** Here are some of the **most common phrasal verbs** in conversation and fiction (*see examples with these verbs on next page*):

Type of Verb	Use	Phrasal Verbs in Conversation and Fiction				
1. **intransitive**	describing actions	come along come over get up shut up sit up come on get out go off sit down stand up				
	other	come off go on run out				
2. **transitive**	actions	get back get in get off pick up set up take off				
	other	give up				

- I think we should **get out** of here.
- It forces you to **sit up** a little bit straighter.
- Ok, I'll **set up** an appointment for lunch.
- Can I **take off** my jacket?

E **Frequency information**. Here are some of the **most common phrasal verbs** in academic writing:

Type of Verb	Use	Phrasal Verbs in Academic Writing			
transitive	actions	*carry out*	*set up*	*take on*	*take up*
	other	*make up*	*point out*		

- Rutherford **carried out** a series of experiments using very thin foils of gold.
- Iron formations **make up** less than one percent of all sedimentary rocks.

Activities

1 **Notice in context:** Read the conversation and the two paragraphs from different types of writing. Circle the phrasal verbs.

1. **Conversation:** *Getting ready to bring out the cake at a birthday party.*

   ELIZABETH: Oh, we're supposed to sit down now?

   BERNARD: Yeah, sit down, Elizabeth.

   ELIZABETH: Okay.

   BERNARD: Come on. Ready, guys? Come on. Everybody has to come.

2. **Fiction writing:** *It's a woman's birthday, but she didn't tell anyone.*

   "I was going to have dinner with the girls tonight." She smiled, but she looked sad. She felt a thousand years old. She hadn't told anyone on the set, but it was her fortieth birthday, and she had had happier ones. "Do you want to come along? We thought we'd go out for hamburgers."

3. **Academic writing:** *Test-taking.*

   When participants arrived at the computer lab to take the test, they completed a consent letter and a questionnaire. All computers had been set up so that the test-takers could start working on the test immediately after receiving instructions.

2 **Practice the meanings:** Choose the correct phrasal verb from the box to complete the meaning of each passage. Write the letter of your choice on the line in front of the item.

> **a.** *go on* (= continue)
> **b.** *point out* (= show)
> **c.** *set up* (= establish)
> **d.** *come on* (= encouragement to leave)
> **e.** *come on* (= encouragement to do something)

_____ **1.** LARA: Cookies go well with milk.

ALMIR: I love these jelly ones. Do you like them?

LARA: Oh they're alright.

ALMIR: They're good. _____, eat one.

_____ **2.** Most students started learning English seriously after entering a private junior and senior high school in Japan. Five levels were _____, depending on the length of time already spent learning English.

_____ **3.** It's alright – just rub it in! _____!

_____ **4.** NENA: Are you hungry?

THANH: I'm beyond hungry!

NENA: Me too. I'm starving!

THANH: _____, let's go get something to eat!

_____ **5.** For many years cigarette manufacturers survived the accusation that cigarettes killed you. Then anti-smoking groups _____ that cigarette smoking was anti-social and could harm friends and family. That damaged the cigarette manufacturers more than you might imagine.

3 **Practice informal writing:** Imagine that you are completing a class project with a friend. Write an email to your friend to talk about the project. Use at least two phrasal verbs common in conversation.

EXAMPLE
When you **get off** work, why don't you **come over** so we can work on the project.

_____

_____

_____

_____

_____

4 **Practice academic writing:** Now write a formal description of the project to hand in to your teacher. Use at least three phrasal verbs that are typical of academic writing.

EXAMPLE
To **carry out** this project, we had to **set up** the experiment.

_____

_____

_____

_____

_____

I can't think of his name now
Verb + Preposition

What have you learned from your grammar textbook?

Transitive phrasal verbs can be **separable**: the verb and particle can be separated by the **object**. But many other **multi-word verbs** occur with a particular **preposition** that must immediately **follow the verb.**

V   O   P_T   V   P_P   O

PHRASAL VERB: I'll ***put** some food **out*** for the cats.   VERB + PREPOSITION: I'll ***wait for** you* right here.

Some **verb + preposition** combinations are called **non-separable transitive phrasal verbs** in some textbooks.

What does the corpus show?

A   **Verb + preposition** combinations are **more common** than separable phrasal verbs. They are common in both conversation and writing.

B   In conversation and fiction writing, the most common verb + preposition combinations are used to express **(1)** actions, **(2)** reported speech, or **(3)** mental states.

    1. I'm ***waiting for*** somebody to come and get me.
    2. I don't like to ***ask for*** money.
    3. I don't ***know about*** that dude.

Frequency information. Here are the **most common verb + preposition** combinations in conversation and fiction:

Use	Verb + Preposition Combinations					
1. actions	*deal with*	*get into*	*go for*	*look at*	*pay for*	*turn to*
	get at	*get over*	*go through*	*look for*	*stare at*	*wait for*
2. reported speech	*ask about*	*ask for*	*speak of*	*speak to*	*talk about*	*talk to*
3. mental states	*believe in*	*know about*	*look into*	*think about*	*worry about*	
	hear of	*listen to*	*look like*	*think of*		

C   Some verbs combine with **several different prepositions** to form multi-word verbs. Each combination has its own special meaning.

Verb + Preposition	Meaning	Example
look at	turn your eyes towards something	• Mary ***looked at*** the visitor.
look for	try to find something	• I started ***looking for*** an escape route.
look into	gaze into something	• She ***looked into*** his eyes with a tired smile.
	investigate	• Bobby hired someone to ***look into*** the accident.
look like	resemble	• His beard made him ***look like*** a cactus.

Verb + Preposition	Meaning	Example
get into [a place]	enter	• I *got into* bed and turned the light off.
get at	try to say	• What are you *getting at*?
get over	recover	• I just can't *get over* it.
think about	consider the possibility	• That's a good idea. I'll *think about* it.
think of	remember or identify	• What did you *think of* him?

D In academic writing, **verb + preposition** combinations often express **(1) causative meanings** or **(2) logical relationships**:

    1. This procedure may *result in* a considerable loss of statistical power.
    2. Most of the population *consisted of* individuals born since 1932.

Many of the most common verb + preposition combinations in writing are **passive**, e.g., *be based on, be associated with* (see Unit 18).

Frequency information. Here are the **most common verb + preposition** combinations in academic writing:

account for	*belong to*	*contribute to*	*depend on*	*lead to*	*refer to*
allow for	*consist of*	*deal with*	*differ from*	*occur in*	*result in*

    • Only 18 grant programs *account for* almost 85 percent of total government spending.
    • Forensic anthropologists seldom *deal with* population level differences.
    • Industrial production *depends on* factories and machinery that generate material goods.
    • The decision to study music or painting could *lead to* trouble.

Activities

1 **Notice in context:** Read the conversation and the paragraph from an academic text. Circle the **verb + preposition** combinations. Some of the verbs are not listed in Sections B-D.

  1. **Conversation:** *About weekend plans.*

     JEN: Alex, you're coming to the picnic right?
     ALEX: No. Well maybe I will. I'll have to think about it.
     JEN: We were talking about cooking Cajun food. You really should come.
     ALEX: I'd like to, but I've been really busy looking for a job.

  2. **Academic writing:** *About international economics.*

    Until recently when commercial farming started in West Africa, the main source of food was small local farms. These local farms account for over 90 per cent of the agricultural output of the country. Since these farms depend on human labor, only small areas of land are cultivated. With the increase in both population and the demand for food, technical and mechanical assistance is needed to allow for an increase in the production levels of the local farms. These topics are dealt with in more detail in Chapters 7 and 8.

2 Analyze discourse: Look back at Activity 1. In the conversation, write in the margin by each **verb + preposition** combination whether it expresses an *action, reported speech,* or a *mental state*. Draw an arrow between the combination and its use. In the paragraph, write *A* (active) or *P* (passive) above each combination.

3 Analyze and edit: These sentences were written by English learners. Decide if each boldfaced verb is correct. If it is correct, write *C* on the line. If it is incorrect, cross it out and write the correct form of the verb on the line.

contribute to   1. I would like to **contribute at** this discussion in order to help find a good solution.

_____   2. That rock **looks as** granite, but it is actually quartzite.

_____   3. For example, there are some societies that don't **allow to** people to drink alcohol.

_____   4. The English language enables us to easily **deal with** others when we travel outside Jordan.

_____   5. I like to hear different topics and **discuss about** them because I believe it improves my English.

_____   6. Competition to produce more natural food will **result** businesses making investments in the improvement of modern technologies.

4 Practice conversation: Read this conversation. Make it sound more natural by replacing the phrases in bold with **verb + preposition** combinations. Write them on the lines. Compare your answers with a partner's.

SANDY: Hey, Mark! What're you doing?

MARK: Uh, just packing. I'm **anticipating** a call from my sister.   _____
We're going to Montana this summer.

SANDY: Montana's beautiful! I **was employed by** a hotel up   _____
there one summer.

MARK: Really? I really need to start **trying to find** work when   _____
I get back. What are you up to all summer?

Now complete the conversation. Include at least two more verb + preposition combinations. When you are finished writing, practice the conversation with a partner.

SANDY: _____
_____

MARK: _____
_____

I have to get out of here
Three-Word Phrasal Verbs

What have you learned from your grammar textbook?

Some phrasal verbs consist of **three words: verb + particle + preposition.** Three-word phrasal verbs are always **transitive** and **nonseparable:**

• He doesn't *get along with* most of his classmates.

What does the corpus show?

A In conversation, the verb *get* **combines with many particles and prepositions** to form different three-word phrasal verbs:

Phrasal Verb with *Get*	Meaning	Example
get away with	do something wrong and not get caught or punished	• You can *get away with* not going to class.
get back to	go back	• I need to *get back to* the office.
	return a phone call	• I told him I'd *get back to* him in a few days.
get back into	begin an activity again	• I'm trying to *get back into* my routine.
get on with	continue, after a problem	• I want to *get on with* my life.
get off at	ending time for work	• She *gets off at* five every night
get off on	begin an activity	• I think I *got off on* the wrong foot.
get off to	begin an activity	• The project is *getting off to* a shaky start.

B The single **most common three-word phrasal verb** is *get out of*. This verb has many different meanings:

Meaning	Examples
1. move to someplace else	• I need to *get out of here* in about five minutes. • He was trying to *get out of sight.*
2. stop interfering with someone	• He should just *get out of my life.* • I'm going to *get out of your hair.*
3. stop doing a regular activity	• They could not *get out of the habit.*
4. avoid doing something	• I'm going to try to *get out of work.*
5. have difficulty breathing	• She *gets out of breath* when she walks.
6. become a problem	• Costs have *gotten out of hand.*

C In conversation and fiction writing, most common three-word phrasal verbs express **actions:**

• I think it just *came out of* the freezer.   • I guess we should *go out for* dinner.

But a few three-word phrasal verbs are common with **non-action** meanings:

• She was *looking forward to* returning home.   • I can't *put up with* the pain.

Frequency information. Here are the **most common three-word phrasal verbs** in conversation and fiction:

action verbs	come in for come out of come out with	get away from get back into get back to	get off at get on with get out of	go along with go out for go over to go up to	turn away from turn back to	catch up with hold on to keep up with look out for
mental verbs	come down to come up with	look forward to	put up with			

D In academic writing, only **two three-word phrasal verbs** are common: *set out in, set up in*. Both of these verbs usually refer to information that is presented in a table, graph, or other kind of display:

- The predicted relationships between the variables are *set out in* Table 4.3.
- The table is *set up in* the form of a financial statement.

Activities

1 **Notice in context:** Read the conversation and the sentences from different types of writing. Circle the three-word phrasal verbs.

1. **Conversation:** *At work.*

   SARA: Last week, Rick was coming out of the office, and he said he heard you were quitting.

   LESLIE: I don't know. I can't keep up with the schedule anymore. The hours are too long.

   SARA: Yeah, the schedule's starting to catch up with all of us. We're all tired.

2. **Fiction writing:**

   a. As soon as he got out of sight, they would hurry away in the other direction, and he would never see them again.

   b. "I've given up my job," he told the guard. "My mother and I are going to the country to get away from things."

   c. Patrick was nearly twenty now, and she couldn't hold on to him forever, she realized that. But she only wanted what was best for him, and letting him go was hard.

3. **Academic writing:**

   a. These project objectives were set out in the first project report and are quoted in Section 2.1.

   b. The Agricultural Training Board was set up in 1966 to improve the technical performance of workers in the industry.

2 **Analyze discourse:** *Get out of* has many different meanings. Read each sentence and use the context to determine the meaning of *get out of*. Show that you understand that meaning by rephrasing the sentence without using *get out of*. Discuss your answers with a classmate.

1. He really needs to **get out of** town and be alone, that's all.
   *He really needs to **leave** town and be alone, that's all.*

2. **Get out of** my chair! I need to sit down.

   _____

3. What day do we finally **get out of** school, John?

_____

4. The only way he could **get out of** the parking ticket was to pay the fine.

_____

5. I had pneumonia and now I **get out of** breath really easily.

_____

6. I understand that Pat is going to **get out of** coaching the baseball team this year. I guess he really just doesn't like it anymore.

_____

7. Don't let the situation **get out of** hand.

_____

8. Ok–just **get out of** my face!

_____

3 **Practice the structure:** Imagine that you have a friend who says everything twice. Below are some of his comments. Guess what your friend will say next. Use a three-word phrasal verb to rephrase each of your friend's comments.

1. I **invented** the entire security system here at the office.

I came up with the entire security system here at the office.

2. Sometimes I like to **escape** the stress of work and get out of town.

_____

3. Even though I move around a lot, I **keep** a lot of my old things.

_____

4. You know, I feel like I **do just as well as** the more experienced workers.

_____

5. My friend Bill and I were **filling each other in on** what we've been up to.

_____

6. Yesterday I **tolerated** three barking dogs all day.

_____

4 **Practice writing a story:** In a fictional story, a writer has to describe the actions of the people in the story. With a classmate, go to a public place, like your classroom, a park, or a market, and write your own story to describe what is happening there. Use three-word phrasal verbs to describe the actions of the people you see.

EXAMPLE

IN A PARK: A small boy is running to **catch up with** a puppy. He reaches out to **hold on to** his tail, but the puppy doesn't seem to want to **put up with** this treatment. He growls as he tries to **get away from** the boy.

_____

_____

_____

No significant difference was found
Passive Voice

Academic Writing

What have you learned from your grammar textbook?

The **passive voice** focuses on the **object** receiving the action. Usually passives occur when the **agent** of an action is **unknown or unimportant**. *(See Unit 17 for the choice between active voice and passives with a by-phrase.)*

Passive Voice
- **The house *was built*** in 1856.

Active Voice
- Someone ***built* the house** in 1856.

What does the corpus show?

A **Passive voice** is much more common in academic writing than in conversation and fiction. It is especially common and useful in research writing, where **omitting the agent** of an action is effective for **several reasons**:

Reason for Omitting the Agent	Passive Voice Example	Active Voice Example
1. Readers **already know the agent** (often "the researchers").	• The production of iron *was measured* over time.	• *Researchers **measured** the production of iron over time.*
2. Passive voice allows the object of the research to be used as the subject of the sentence, **giving more importance to the object** than to the researchers.	• **Three plant communities on a marsh *were exposed*** to elevated carbon dioxide concentrations . . .	• *We **exposed** three plant communities on a marsh to elevated carbon dioxide concentrations . . .*
3. Passive voice contributes to a **greater sense of objectivity**, because human actions are not mentioned.	• No significant difference *was found* between the two groups.	• *We **found** no significant difference between the two groups.*

B **Frequency information.** **Passive voice** verbs are especially **common** for **two functions** in research writing:

Common Function of Passive Voice	Most Common Passive Voice Verbs and Expressions			
1. **describing methods** and analyses	*be analyzed* *be calculated* *be carried out*	*be collected* *be measured* *be observed*	*be obtained* *be prepared* *be set*	*be tested* *be used*
2. **reporting findings**, or **interpreting** their meaning and connection with other research	*be determined* *be expected*	*be found* *be seen*	*be shown*	*be associated with* *be believed to be* *can be interpreted as*

- A large-scale experiment was ***carried out*** in which cold sea water was injected into lava flows.
- A solvent ***was used*** to separate larger quantities of the silica gel.

- The absolute level of cooperativeness for urban subjects ***was found*** to be quite high.
- The parallel arrangement of nuclear moments ***is shown*** in Figure 2.12.

C Be careful! Even though **passive verbs** are more common in academic writing than in conversation and other types of writing, they account for **only about ¼ of the verbs**. Overuse of passive voice can make writing less effective. Even in research writing, professionals **use active voice** with names or personal pronouns to **describe some actions and interpretations**:

- *Zotkin and Tsikulin measured* the angle of 40,000 fallen trees.
- *We interpret* these results in the following way: . . .

Sometimes writers **use active voice** because they want to **emphasize the researcher's role** (for example, in a new procedure or with a new interpretation).

However, **different academic fields** have **different expectations for the use of passive voice**. For instance, some fields always report procedures in passive voice; in other fields there is great variation. Discuss the expectations for your academic field with your teachers.

Activities

1 Notice in context: Read this paragraph about research. Underline the passive voice verbs and circle the subjects of those verbs.

How to Conduct Interviews for Research

Many types of data can be easily gathered. Research is more problematic if the data are collected from personal interviews. Before people are interviewed, the interviewers should be given some training, since only trained interviewers can carry out the process accurately. In some situations, the social and psychological aspects of interviews are too often ignored. For example, the use of white interviewers in a black community may distort the information. Great care must be taken with the interview respondents, since they are very important to the research project.

2 Practice writing: These sentences describe a research project that studied plants. Each pair has one sentence in passive voice and one in active voice. Choose one sentence from each pair so that together your four choices make an effective paragraph. Circle the letter of your choice.

Dangers to Growing Plants Are Seen in Leaf Development

1. **a.** Some of the dangers to plants can be measured by studying individual leaves or flowers or seeds.
   b. Botanists can measure dangers to plants by studying individual leaves or flowers or seeds.

2. **a.** White clover was chosen as an ideal plant to study in order to observe threats to plant life.
   b. Many people thought white clover would be a good plant to study in order to observe threats to plant life.

3. **a.** In a field study, young leaves were marked as they began to expand, and their development was followed by repeated observation.
   b. In a field study, Peters marked young leaves as they began to expand and then followed their development by repeated observation.

4. **a.** From this, some of the causes of death or damage in plant populations were determined.
   b. From this he determined some of the causes of death or damage in plant populations.

(continued on next page)

Concluding Sentence: In the future, plant leaves will be studied carefully, since they contain important clues about plant health.

Now write your paragraph, adding the concluding sentence above. Then compare your paragraph with a partner's. Discuss your reasons for choosing passive or active voice for sentences 1 to 4, and explain the author's choice in the concluding sentence.

_____

_____

_____

_____

_____

_____

3 **Practice writing:** Use the notes in the box to write a paragraph about the scientific study of insects. For each sentence you write, choose between active and passive voice. Use some of the common passive voice verbs listed in Section B.

> • the scientific study of insects = "entomology"
> • over a million species of insects observed in wild
> • perhaps four million species more
> • insects in nearly all environments
> • only a few types of insects in oceans
> • many believe insects are one of the most abundant types of life

_____

_____

_____

_____

_____

_____

When you are done, compare your paragraph with a partner's. Explain the choices you made between active and passive verbs.

What have you learned from your grammar textbook?

Passive sentences usually do not tell us who the agent is (*see Unit 16*). When it is **important to give the identity of the agent**, a ***by*-phrase** can be used with the passive verb:

passive verb + *by*-phrase (= agent)

- His insurance coverage ***was provided by*** his wife's employer.

What does the corpus show?

A A sentence with a *by*-passive means almost the same thing as a sentence with an active voice verb because both sentences identify the agent. There are **three main reasons** why we **use a *by*-passive** instead of an active voice verb. Many *by*-passive sentences fit more than one reason.

Reason to Use a *By*-Passive	Example
1. The agent noun phrase is **long**.	• She ***had been neglected by*** nurses who had no time to spend cheering up an old woman.
2. The agent is "**new**" information.	• The cancellation ***was disclosed by*** Randall Robinson, head of a private group with close ties to the Angola government.
3. The main verb belongs to a special group of verbs that are often used with **non-human** *by*-phrases.	• The firm's credit standing ***was supported by*** strong retail franchises and an "acceptable level" of risk-adjusted capital.

B When the **agent** noun phrase is **short**, it is usually the **subject of an active** voice verb:

- *They **neglected** you in the old days.*

But if the **agent** noun phrase is **long**, we usually express the agent as a ***by*-phrase with a passive** verb:

- It ***was signed by*** presidents Vinicio Cerezo of Guatemala, Rafael Angel Calderon of Costa Rica, Leonardo Callejas of Honduras, and Violeta Chamorro of Nicaragua.

C Sentences usually have both "old" information and "new" information. The "old" information refers to people or things that readers are already familiar with. **"New" information** has **not been previously mentioned** in the text, and is **not widely known**. It is usually **more important** than the "old" information.

In general, writers prefer to put old information as the subject of a sentence, and **new information at the end of a sentence**. Therefore, if the **agent is "new"** information, we use a ***by*-passive** to put it at **the end of the sentence**. Thus, "Customs agents" is the new information below:

- Avelino was found innocent of all charges. He ***had been entrapped by*** Customs agents.

D The ***by*-passive** is especially **common with particular verbs** in academic writing. These verbs are special because the ***by*-phrase** usually identifies a kind of **data or evidence**, rather than a human agent:

- The amount of profit in the economy ***is determined by*** the amount of surplus value created within it.

In many cases, the ***by*-phrase** with these verbs contains a **gerund clause**:

- Isomerism may ***be explained by assuming*** that the atoms are arranged in a definite manner.

Frequency information. Here is a list of **passive voice verbs** that commonly occur **with a non-human** *by*-**phrase** in academic writing:

be accompanied by	be described by	be illustrated by	be replaced by
be caused by	be determined by	be influenced by	be represented by
be characterized by	be explained by	be measured by	be shown by
be confirmed by	be found by	be obtained by	be supported by
be defined by	be given by		

- The home range can then **be determined by** studying the distribution of droppings.
- The causes can **be illustrated by** considering a simple eccentric wheel model.
- Long term profit expectations **are influenced by** technological progress.

Activities

1 **Notice in context:** Read this paragraph from an academic text about diseases in Europe. Circle the passive verbs and underline the agent of each verb.

An account of the spread of cholera through Asia and Europe in the 1830s is given by Walker (1983) and continues to be relevant even today. Today a threat which creates much concern in the United Kingdom is rabies, and it was highlighted by the decision to build a Channel tunnel, directly connecting the UK to the rest of Europe. Rabies was successfully eradicated from the UK at the turn of the century by national efforts; however, the threat of importation of the disease has returned.

2 **Analyze discourse:** Read these passages from academic writing. Complete each one with an active or a *by*-passive form of the verb in parentheses. Compare your responses with a partner's. Give a reason for each response.

1. The Education Act in Scotland was passed in 1872. The ability to read complicated texts could not be assumed in all children, even from respectable families. This fact _____ the
   (illustrate)

   remarks of the owner of a paper factory in 1873. He said that not one of his children workers was able to read the Bible correctly

2. Some scientists observe the experiences that an animal has, and study how the animal's actions depend on its experiences. They insist that an animal's actions _____ past experiences
   (influence)

   as well as present ones. They accept that experience does change the state of the brain.

3. A calendar of events is a time schedule for carrying out the required tasks of the research project. It _____ the detailed organization necessary for convincing an academic
   (represent)

   advisor that the project is feasible; it is also another indication of how carefully and realistically the proposal has been developed.

4. The flight movements of insects _____ three sets of muscles: the indirect,
   (cause)

   direct, and accessory direct muscles. The indirect muscles are usually the largest in the body and are not directly attached to the wings.

3 **Practice writing:** The following passages are all grammatically correct; however, the boldfaced sentences need to be rephrased to make them more appropriate for academic writing. Rephrase them by changing active verbs to *by*-passives and *by*-passives to active verbs. Write each one on the line provided. Then discuss with a partner why each verb was changed.

1. In West Africa there are four types of vegetation, including the high forest in the south. **A wide range of trees suitable for fuel-wood characterizes the forest.** In the savannah area there is less vegetation with fewer trees. The limited availability of suitable fuel-wood has contributed to the use of less suitable materials as fuel.

   _____

   _____

2. The lecture as a form of communication in higher education has been strongly criticized, especially by students. **Yet, that lectures do have considerable appeal for students has been shown by a recent investigation.** Both students and lecturers said that they felt that lectures gave an opportunity for personal contact.

   _____

   _____

3. To combat the further spread of disease, general newspaper advertising started during March 1986. Then began a campaign of posters, radio and television. **A national telephone information and advice service supported this effort.**

   _____

   _____

4. The study used letters written between Poles in the USA and their families at home in Poland to analyze progress integrating into American culture. A total of 754 letters were purchased and the results were analyzed in groups of family names. **Advertising in a Polish-American magazine published in the USA obtained the letters.**

   _____

   _____

Further details can be found in . . .
Passive Verb + Preposition

Informational Writing

What have you learned from your grammar textbook?

Passive voice verbs can be followed by a prepositional phrase that expresses the agent of the action (*see Unit 17*). These prepositional phrases use ***by***:

- This table ***was made by*** my grandfather.

What does the corpus show?

A In informational writing (newspaper and academic writing), certain **passive verb + preposition** combinations are very **common**. These combinations use prepositions other than *by*.

Frequency information. Here is a list of **common passive verb + preposition** combinations in informational writing:

Preposition	Common Passive Verb + Preposition Combinations		
as	*be classified as* *be considered as*	*be defined as* *be known as*	*be referred to as* *be regarded as*
in	*be found in* *be included in*	*be involved in* *be shown in*	*be used in*
to	*be applied to* *be attributed to*	*be confined to* *be linked to*	*be related to*
Other prepositions	*be associated with* *be based on*	*be composed of* *be derived from*	*be required for* *be used for*

B **Passive verb + preposition** combinations fulfill **important functions for writing**. These are **four of the most common functions** and their most common combinations:

Function + Most Common Combinations	Description of Use	Examples
1. **identifying places** *be found in* *be shown in*	• identifies places within texts and physical locations • sometimes used to explain where evidence for an argument is located • ***be found in*** often occurs with ***can***, implying that everyone has the ability to find the information	• More than 90 minerals including gold, silver, and copper ***are found in*** Kazakhstan. • The breakdown of the budget ***is shown in*** Table 2. • The economic expansions in America are larger than the contractions. Proof of this ***can be found in*** a comparison of America in 1915 and 1985.
2. **classifying, naming, defining** *be classified as* *be known as* *be referred to as*	• tells a category for something, provides a name, or defines a term	• This bike ride ***is classified as*** moderate and has a long, downhill run back to Santa Cruz. • The unit of study ***is known as*** a "case" and ***is referred to as*** "n" in research reports.

Function + Most Common Combinations	Description of Use	Examples
3. **connecting ideas, data, conclusions** *be associated with be based on be related to*	• some expressions connect two ideas • ***be based on*** identifies the evidence for research or the background for something	• There is no clear evidence that dust *is associated with* the passage of disease. • Part 8 of this report *is based on* a questionnaire survey. • Every problem *is related to* a larger world.
4. **identifying uses, applications** *be applied to be used in*	• identifies how something can be used	• The idea of disorder can *be applied to* molecules. • Computer chips *are used in* everything from personal computers to microwave ovens.

Activities

1 **Notice in context:** Read this news report about airport noise. Circle the **passive verb + preposition** combinations.

Pilots, airlines and community groups have agreed on a drastic noise reduction plan for Seattle-Tacoma International Airport, which is known as "Sea-Tac." Irene Jones, a community leader, said the agreement could cut noise in half. However, no specific action is required for the immediate future. Major airlines also have been looking for clear standards on noise levels at airports, as well as a timetable for eliminating older, noisier airliners. Neither is found in the new policy.

2 **Analyze discourse:** Read these examples of informational writing. Underline all the **passive verb + preposition** combinations that are used as main verbs. Then describe the function of each passive verb + preposition combination (using the information in Section B). Be as specific as possible. Write your description on the line.

1. The loss of heat <u>is shown in</u> Figure 2.3.   *indentifies a place within the text*

2. The occupations were classified as unskilled, or semi-skilled, so it is no surprise to find that they were almost always badly paid. _____

3. Lycra is Du Pont's trade name for the elastic fiber spandex. It is used in such clothing as swimsuits and leotards. _____

4. Three major manufacturers, Krups, Braun, and Sanyo, have recently introduced versions of juice extractors that can be found in most department and cooking stores. These units perform well and are easy to clean. _____

5. The results presented in this chapter are based on 624 completed student questionnaires returned by the organizers of 55 advanced courses. _____

6. The now-defunct secret police agency was known as DINA. The woman admitted she is a former agent, and said she traveled to the United States under the assumed name of Liliana Walker.
_____

3 **Practice the structure:** Complete these informational passages with the correct prepositions after the passive verbs.

1. The Chewong are a hunter-gatherer people who are found _____ the tropical rain forest of the Malay Peninsula. Linguistically and culturally they are related _____ the Semai people. The Malaysian aboriginals are usually classified _____ non-violent, non-aggressive, and peaceful.

2. A long message from the Eagle Snack Company's president is included _____ the Cape Cod Potato Chip package. It states the benefits of using canola oil and is linked _____ an offer to replace the product if consumers aren't satisfied. A bar graph is found _____ the package, comparing the saturated-fat content of its canola oil with sunflower oil, corn oil, and soybean oil. Eagle's use of canola oil is confined _____ its Cape Cod Chips sold in the Pacific Northwest. An official of Eagle Snacks said it's unclear how much canola oil might be used _____ other products. The decision to use other ingredients will be based _____ consumer interest in lower levels of saturated fats.

4 **Practice writing:** Rewrite each sentence using the **passive verb + preposition** combination in parentheses. Use the correct form of **be** in each sentence.

1. Look in Chapter Two for a population graph.

   _____
   (can be found in)

2. People think hot weather is common in August.

   _____
   (be regarded as)

3. We had interviews with five people to obtain data.

   _____
   (be involved in)

4. Scientists call the mammoth a prehistoric animal.

   _____
   (be classified as)

That's an important thing to know
The Nouns *People* and *Thing*

What have you learned from your grammar textbook?

Nouns can be **count nouns** (e.g., *girl-girls*) or **noncount nouns** (e.g., *sugar*), and some count nouns have irregular plurals (e.g., *man-men, tooth-teeth*).

Nouns and **pronouns** are related parts of speech. Pronouns can be used in place of a noun:

- I'm going to Virginia to see *my sister. She*'s been in the hospital.

What does the corpus show?

A   In academic writing, **nouns** are by far the **most common part of speech**. No individual noun is especially common. Rather, an author will use different nouns depending on the subject matter of the text.

B   In conversation, nouns are much less frequent. In fact, there are **more pronouns than nouns** in conversation.

NICKI:	Well *I* would like to start **tomorrow morning** at eight o'clock.
SALLY:	OK.
NICKI:	*It*'s probably gonna be a pretty grueling **day**.
JACK:	*I* would expect so . . . *I* want to get started right now.
NICKI:	Well *we* can talk about *that* then. Um let *me* ask . . . See, some of *us* have read some of the **material** and some of *us* haven't.

People in conversation use pronouns instead of nouns because they are familiar with each other's friends and normal activities.

C   Although nouns are generally rare in conversation, **two individual nouns are especially common**: *people* and *thing*. The use of these two simple nouns is more complicated than you might guess.

D   The **plural** noun *people* is the **most common noun** in conversation. The noun *people* usually does NOT refer to a specific set of persons. Rather, we use *people* when we mean "everyone," especially when we make a general statement about life:

- *People* are always saying you have to go to college.   • Lots of *people* have done it wrong.

E   The **singular** noun *thing* is almost **as frequent as *people*** in conversation. The plural noun *things* is less common and is used for imprecise reference (*see Unit 20*). *Thing* can refer to a physical object, but that meaning is rare. Rather, *thing* **has several special functions** in conversation:

Function	Examples
1. referring to an **event** or **activity**	• *The first thing* you got to do is to read the book.
2. referring to a **speech** or **communication** (what someone *said, heard, saw, knew,* or *noticed*)	• *The other thing* I *said* was that she has to be home at five o'clock. • *The last thing* I *heard* was that this guy had asked her out. • That reminds me of *a thing* I *saw* on *Monty Python* once.

(continued on next page)

Function	Examples
3. referring to a **general situation**—the speaker often uses an adjective to express his/her attitude about it	• It's *a good thing* you caught it. • *The funny thing* is both of you are never home. • Candy is *the last thing* I need, Ben! [= *I do not need candy.*] • *The most important thing* is that they have to be able to get along together.
4. telling the listener that the speaker is **making an important point**	• Well, *the thing is* that I can't work the clutch with sandals. • *The only thing is* that I have to have all of this stuff done at the same time.

Activities

1 **Notice in context:** Read the two conversations. Circle each instance of *people* and each instance of *thing*.

1. *Telling a story about a trip to the museum.*

   ELLEN: We were waiting in line forever, and this girl jumped over the rope in line by these tourists in front of us and said, "Oh, I'm with them. I'm their tour guide."

   ANDY: That's so rude! People really make me mad sometimes.

2. *Talking about plans for an outdoor concert to raise money for cancer research.*

   JACK: Did you talk to Bob yesterday about the fundraiser he's putting on?

   DANA: The only thing I said to Bob is that we are totally behind you. There's free food, too.

   NATE: Really? That's the one nice thing about it.

   JACK: Uh, I'll be out of town; I'll miss the whole thing.

   NATE: Oh, but the thing is, it's like ten degrees. Way too cold!

2 **Analyze discourse:** Look back at the conversations in Activity 1. Write what each circled word refers to in the margin. Use one of the labels below. Draw an arrow between the word and the label.

   a. everyone
   b. event / activity
   c. speech / communication
   d. general situation
   e. important point

3 **Practice conversation:** These dialogues don't sound very natural. Replace the boldfaced nouns or noun phrases with *people* or *thing* to make the dialogues sound more natural. You will usually need to include modifiers with *thing*. When you are finished, practice these dialogues with a partner.

1. PAUL: When **individuals** get married and have families,   _____*people*_____
              money does become more important.

   BRAD: But it's not **the factor that is most important**.   _____

2. JEFF: **The result we do not want is to** irritate our boss with too many questions. _____

DAN: Yeah, I was thinking **the identical thought**, but how else do we know what he wants us to do? _____

JEFF: I have no idea.

3. PAM: See, **that's the single behavior** I don't understand. _____

JIM: What's that?

PAM: Why do **drivers in general** need to take up the _____
whole road? Why can't they just let
other drivers pass? _____

4 **Practice conversation:** Answer the questions using **_people_** or **_thing_** in your responses. Write at least two responses for each question.

1. What thoughts or beliefs are common in your city or country?

Lots of **people** believe that thirteen is an unlucky number.

_____

_____

2. What do you do before you go to bed every night?

_____

_____

3. What characteristics make a good co-worker or classmate?

_____

_____

I love fitness and stuff like that
Imprecise Noun Phrases

What have you learned from your grammar textbook?

Nouns and pronouns are parts of speech that refer to people, places, and things. **(1) Personal pronouns** can be used in place of a noun. **(2) Indefinite pronouns** are used when the speaker does not want to specify an exact reference.

1. I'm going to Virginia to see *my sister*. *She*'s been in the hospital.
2. He said *something* about her father.

What does the corpus show?

A In **conversation**, speakers commonly use **imprecise noun phrases**, because they don't have time to be exact. The listeners usually have no trouble understanding the meaning. **Three grammatical devices** are especially important: **(1) indefinite pronouns**, **(2)** the nouns *things* and *stuff*, and **(3) coordination tags**.

B **Indefinite pronouns** that correspond to *people* and *thing* (*see Unit 19*) are often used for **imprecise reference** in conversation. The pronoun *something* is especially common.

	Indefinite Pronouns				Examples
people	*anybody* *anyone*	*everybody* *everyone*	*somebody* *someone*	*nobody* *no one*	• *Somebody* said I looked quite pale today. • Let's try to get *everyone* together to go bowling.
thing	*anything*	*everything*	*something*	*nothing*	• I'll do *anything* you want. • Well, it's better than *nothing*.

C The **plural** noun *things* and the **noncount** noun *stuff* are also commonly used for **imprecise reference** in conversation:

  • And there are other *things* that it can do.   • I might leave some of this *stuff* at my mom's house.

This use of *things* is **different** from the use of singular *thing* (*see Unit 19*).

D In conversation, speakers often use **coordination tags** to show that they have **not exactly identified the noun** that they are thinking of:

  • You don't need to use the computer *or anything*.   • He had been in the war *and all that*.

Frequency information. Here is a list of the **most common coordination tags** in conversation:

Coordination Tag	Meaning	Examples
or something (like that)	the preceding noun is not exactly what the speaker meant	• It costs like fifty bucks *or something*. • He covered his head with a pillow *or something like that*.
and things (like that)	there are additional unstated nouns that should be added to the preceding noun	• It happens a lot that they get like really violent and make threats *and things*. • Don't we have a Master of Fine Arts in drawing *and things like that*?

Coordination Tag	Meaning	Examples
and stuff (like that)	there are additional unstated nouns that should be added to the preceding noun	• Are you taking hiking boots *and stuff*? • You can't really go on trips *and stuff like that*.

Activities

1 **Notice in context:** Read the conversation. Circle the indefinite pronouns, underline the imprecise nouns, and double underline the coordination tags.

At the end of a semester.

NIKKI: Did you ask our professor when we're getting our grades for sure?

DANA: I've been trying every day. I'll ask again tomorrow. I have to go in the morning and finish some things on campus. I don't even know if anyone will be there tomorrow.

NIKKI: I'd come with you, but, I have to run some errands and stuff like that, and I also have to take that job application downtown. Then I'm pretty much free.

2 **Analyze discourse:** Read these excerpts from different conversations. Match each boldfaced word or phrase with the appropriate meaning from the box. Discuss with a partner why the speaker used an imprecise noun phrase in each example.

> **a.** other activities that I shouldn't have done
> **b.** good snacks
> **c.** interesting places
> **d.** another period of time
> **e.** a place to live
> **f.** problems

___c___ **1.** We bought a hiking book about New Mexico and Arizona, and they've got so much **stuff** in those states. There's just a lot to do.

_____ **2.** Well, my mom knows I act differently around different people. Like, I've probably never gotten in trouble with Katy, because Katy doesn't do anything, but, yeah, I've come home late and **stuff like that**, but nothing really bad.

_____ **3.** The last time they brought the snacks for the meeting they had cookies and vegetables and **stuff like that**. I mean, it was a lot nicer than chips and crackers.

_____ **4.** JANE: I mean, it's an old house. Well, we worked on it, cleaned it up, and now we're trying to sell the house and then look for **something** nice.

LINDA: Where?

JANE: I don't know. Just around here.

_____ **5.** DANNY: So many **things** can happen with this microphone, you know. It's pretty old.

JOHN: So is it working now?

DANNY: Yeah, but the batteries died, so now I have to switch the batteries.

_____ **6.** MOLLY: How long did that drought last? A year or **something like that**?

LAURA: Ten years, actually.

3 **Practice conversation:** Imagine that you have just returned home from a weekend at the beach with some friends. Your roommate asks you about your trip, but you are too tired to give long or detailed answers. Answer the questions using imprecise noun phrases in each response. Write at least two responses for each question. When you are finished, practice the questions and answers with a partner.

1. What kinds of things did you do at the beach?

    You know, we went swimming **and stuff like that.**

    _____

    _____

2. What souvenirs did you bring home?

    _____

    _____

3. I heard it was crowded at the beach this weekend. Who else was there?

    _____

    _____

UNIT 21

The chair of the committee
Nonsexist Language Choices

What have you learned from your grammar textbook?

(1) Traditionally, singular nouns with generic reference and indefinite pronouns (such as *someone*) take the **singular pronoun he** (or *his* or *him*), even though they refer to males and females. **(2)** Sometimes in **informal English**, indefinite pronouns are used with **plural pronouns** to avoid using a male pronoun.

1. *A student of English* has a difficult job; *he* has to learn many exceptions to rules.
2. If I told *someone*, *they* would laugh.

What does the corpus show?

A In generic references, there are **many strategies for avoiding words that refer to a male or female**. Some individuals have a single favorite strategy, but there are also some general patterns in conversation and writing. The following are four common strategies.

B The first strategy is using **gender-neutral terms** for **jobs**:

Description of Use	Examples
• Rather than using traditional male terms such as *chairman* and *businessman*, some job names are used with **-person** or **-people**. These terms are used in both conversation and writing. • The three most common nouns with *-person* are: **chairperson, salesperson**, and **spokesperson**. • The noun **chair** is often used in place of *chairperson* or *chairman*, even when the sex of the person is known.	• We want to have a **spokesperson** from each group. (CONV.) • At Ethan Allen furniture stores, **salespeople** are called "designers." (NEWS) • Send a letter to Ray, who is officially the **chair** of the committee. (CONV.)
• Other traditional terms that specified a sex, such as *steward/stewardess*, *waiter/waitress*, and *postman*, have new neutral terms such as **flight attendant, server**, and **letter carrier**. • Although the older terms still occur occasionally (usually in conversation), the new terms are widely used.	• Airline pilots, **flight attendants**, and machinists said they were prepared to negotiate. (NEWS) • Our **server** didn't happen to come back did she? I wanted some ketchup. (CONV.)

C The second strategy is using **plural pronouns** for **singular indefinite references**:

Description of Use	Examples
• This strategy is most common in conversation, but some writers also choose to use it even though it violates traditional grammar rules.	• If *anybody* wants the picture, *they* can get if off the computer disk. (CONV.) • If there is *someone* whose work you admire, then use *them* as a role model. (ACAD.)

D The third strategy is using **plural nouns** for **generic reference:**

Description of Use	Example
• In both conversation and writing, people use plural nouns for generic references. The use of the plural pronoun *they* is then consistent with formal grammar rules.	• While *teachers* command social respect in Nicaragua, *they* are not near the top of the salary scale. (ACAD.)

E The fourth strategy is using **the combinations *he or she* and *he/she*:**

Description of Use	Examples
• These combinations are rare, probably because they are awkward to read. They most often occur in academic writing.	• *The caller* has to ask for the telephone extension *he or she* requires. (ACAD.) • Reassure *your language helper* every now and then that you appreciate correction. Remember that *he/she* is a human being who gets tired. (ACAD.)

Activities

1 **Notice in context:** This academic text illustrates a variety of generic references. Find the nouns and pronouns that refer to people. Underline them if they represent a nonsexist language choice. Circle them if they use a traditional male term for generic reference.

The most typical approach used by door-to-door salespeople is to introduce themselves: "Good morning, I'm Joe Smith, from the Zed company." No matter what approach a salesperson adopts with his or her potential customers, it is an important step, since a customer's likelihood of listening to a salesman in the next few minutes depends on the sales agent's success in arousing that person's interest. However, this is not an easy task: Stopping someone in the street or knocking on someone's door is already an intrusion on their freedom.

2 **Analyze discourse:** Match each sentence with a nonsexist strategy from the box. Be careful: one sentence reflects two strategies.

a. A plural pronoun that refers to a previous indefinite pronoun	**c.** Plural noun + plural pronoun for generic reference
b. A gender-neutral term for a job	**d.** A combination of male and female pronouns

_____ **1.** **Firefighters** do a lot of lifting, don't **they**? Wouldn't you imagine that **they** do a lot? Those hoses are heavy.

_____ **2.** If, um, you know, you help **someone** and **they** say thank you and **they** smile, it's contagious and it's gonna make you feel good.

_____ **3.** Students need to feel a sense of belonging. The burden of each person's school success should not rest on **his/her** shoulders alone.

_____ **4.** The film begins when Milly and Clara enter the kitchen of their family home, where their mother and a **cameraperson** are already present.

3 **Practice non-sexist terms:** Read these excerpts from conversations or newspapers. Change the boldfaced traditional terms to nonsexist terms. Cross out the traditional term and write the nonsexist one above it. Make all necessary changes, such as verb agreement.

1. If someone is speaking English with me and **~~he messes~~** <u>they mess</u> up the verb "to be," I don't care. "Um, he, he are, he are going to the store." I still know what **he** means. (CONV.)

2. **A teacher** can be barred from the classroom for one year for neglecting **his** duty by going on strike. (NEWS)

3. A Corrections Department **spokesman** says the inmate will have twenty minutes before the parole board. (NEWS)

4. Here's how CarBargains works: A **man** would call the CarBargains staff and describe the make, model and style of car for which **he** was looking. (NEWS)

5. Carol is the admissions **chairman** of the Math and Science Department. (CONV.)

4 **Practice writing:** Complete a newspaper report about a fire that broke out in a local department store. Use nonsexist terms to describe the people involved in this event. Remember, the second strategy (Section C) is not typical of informational writing, but it is likely to be common in quotations.

Yesterday during the lunch hour, flames were seen on the roof of Gordon's Department Store.
Servers from the store's restaurant called in an alarm at 12:37 pm. . . .

_____

_____

_____

_____

_____

The introduction of technology
The Definite Article

What have you learned from your grammar textbook?

The **definite article**, *the,* is used before a noun when the speaker and listener both know the specific person or thing that is referred to. The definite article occurs because (**1**) the **noun** was **already mentioned**, (**2**) the noun refers to a **person/thing that is unique**, (**3**) an **adjective** such as *best* **identifies the noun**, or (**4**) the **context makes it clear** what the noun refers to.

1. I saw a dog, and behind *the dog* there was a cat.
2. *The sun* is hot today.
3. She won *the best prize*.
4. He went to *the library*.

What does the corpus show?

A   The **definite article** sometimes occurs because a **referent** (person or thing referred to) was **already mentioned** in a text, but this use accounts for only about 1/4 of all occurrences of *the* in conversation and writing. **Other reasons for using the definite article** include the following:

Reason	Description of Use	Examples
1. The referent is known from the **shared context**.	• most common reason in conversation • sometimes the referent is in the immediate environment • the referent can also be a shared part of people's lives, such as their pet dog	• Give me *the butter*, please. • Bob, put *the dog* out, would you please?
2. The referent is **specified** by **modifiers** of the noun.	• most common reason in informational writing • often, the modifiers come **after** the noun (i.e., a prepositional phrase or relative clause) • sometimes the modifiers are adjectives **before** the noun	• *The introduction* of technology into teaching should include support and training. (ACAD.) • The midwestern states had *the most affordable* **homes**. (NEWS)
3. The referent **can be inferred** from a noun that was previously mentioned.	• common in writing • sometimes the inference is simple, such as recognizing a new noun as a synonym for a previous noun • sometimes the inference requires making more complex connections	• *Fifty-five children* were enrolled in this study. *The patients* were . . . (ACAD.) • Below us, an old pale blue *Ford* rattled into view. *The driver* swung wide around my car . . . (FICT.) [The driver is a definite noun because the reader is expected to know that a Ford is a kind of car and that moving cars have drivers.]
4. New people, things, or events are **presented as** though they are **familiar**.	• especially in fiction • this technique is used to get readers involved in the story	• When *the call* first came in from Fraxilly, I didn't accept it. [beginning of a novel]

B Frequency information. Here is a list of the **most common reasons for the use of the definite article** in conversation and different types of writing:

Most Common Reason for Definite Article Use	Conversation	Fiction	Informational Writing
a. introduced previously in text	25%	30%	25–30%
b. shared situational context	55%	10%	10%
c. modifiers of the noun	5%	15%	30–40%
d. inference	5%	10%	15%
e. other	10%	35%	10%

Other reasons include idioms and generic reference. In some cases (especially in fiction), the reason for a definite article cannot be analyzed with certainty.

Activities

1 Notice in context: In these excerpts from different academic texts, the use of definite articles is based on each noun being specified by modifiers. Circle the definite articles, underline nouns once, and underline the modifiers twice.

1. *From a report about cattle in England.*

   The east of England had the lowest number of beef herds and the smallest herds.

2. *From a book about second language learning.*

   The main emphasis during the early stages of language learning is on pronunciation.

3. *From an article about evolution.*

   The bend in the lower spine of humans which is responsible for so many back pains exists because our ancestors were quadrupeds, and we have only recently started standing upright.

2 Analyze discourse: Read the report and the conversation. Circle all the definite articles. Above each one, write the number of the reason (*R1–R4*) for using the definite article. Use the chart in Section A to decide which reason applies. Sometimes more than one reason can apply.

1. **Academic writing:** *Personal report about what it is like to be a student with physical disabilities.*

   There are issues which still concern me about continuing education for students with disabilities, for example, the fear and ignorance that often surround this condition known as "disability," and the prejudice and stereotyping of people who do not "fit" into a mythical category commonly known as "normal."

2. **Conversation:** *Between women who have been friends since high school.*

   RAMONA: I don't even remember what I did at the graduation party, what did we do?
   ALICIA: We didn't do anything.
   RAMONA: We had fun at the after-party at Angie's house though.
   ALICIA: That was the best party! You were only there for a little while, I think.

3 **Analyze and edit:** Read each excerpt. The boldfaced part contains an error in the use of the definite article. Correct the error and rewrite the boldfaced part on the line.

1. *In a restaurant.*

   MELI: Did we pay already?

   THANH: Not yet. **Our bill is here on a table.**

   _____

2. Sometimes it is not possible to decide when we have a satisfactory answer to a problem, or **even when we have a best answer.**

   _____

3. I will talk about **some of problems I would be faced with** if I suddenly had to live in a foreign country.

   _____

4. First Interstate reported a $59.9 million loss for the two previous quarters, **as bank continued to be hurt by bad real estate loans.**

   _____

4 **Practice writing:** Write an informational paragraph describing some of the experiences that people have when they start learning English. Use definite articles in the ways that are typical for informational writing.

The first time that new learners go to English class, they are often discouraged. The learners . . .

_____

_____

_____

_____

_____

Yeah, that's right!
The Pronouns *This* and *That*

What have you learned from your grammar textbook?

(1) The pronouns ***this*** and ***these*** refer to things that are **near** to you. (2) The pronouns ***that*** and ***those*** refer to things that are **away** from you.

> 1. *Mom, **this** is a really good salad.*

> 2. ***That** is a nice beach.*

What does the corpus show?

A **Frequency information.** In **conversation**, the pronoun ***that*** is **extremely common**, but the pronoun *this* is not frequent.

In **academic writing**, neither pronoun is especially frequent, but the pronoun ***this*** is **twice as common** as *that*.

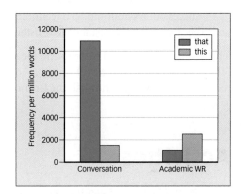

B The pronoun ***that*** usually does **NOT** refer to a specific object or person that is distant from the speaker. Rather, ***that*** is **common in conversation** because it has **several special functions**:

Function	Common Pattern	Examples
1. **evaluating an idea** or **a situation**	***that's*** + **adjective** *bad good right* *cool great too bad* *fine nice true* *funny okay*	**A:** We see those cactus a lot around our house. **B:** Yeah, ***that's nice.*** **A:** I slept fine. I didn't hear a thing. **B:** Well ***that's good.***
	that's + **noun phrase**	**A:** Well there wouldn't be any problems if not for science. **B:** That is true. ***That's a good point.***
	that sounds + **adjective**	**A:** Well maybe that should be a suggestion for a Christmas present. **B:** OK. ***That sounds good.***
2. **summarizing the main point** of the preceding statements	***that's*** + ***wh*-clause** *what where how* *when why*	**A:** I've been trying to call Tony every day this week. **B:** Oh, he's been out of town. **A:** OK, so tell him ***that's why I've been leaving messages for him.***
3. as part of a **coordination tag***	***or something like that***	• She always had a big dish of some kind of preserves, figs or peaches ***or something like that.***

*For more on coordination tags, *see Unit 20.*

C In **academic writing**, the pronoun *this* is **much more common** than *that*. *This* almost never refers to a specific object that is near. Rather, the pronoun *this* usually **refers to the idea expressed in the preceding sentences**:

• Loban (1963) was able to highlight one crucial problem. He found that the frequency of dependent clauses in the written language of high-ability students did not increase, while it did for low-ability children. *This* suggests that there is a ceiling to the effectiveness of such frequency counts.

Be careful! When you use the pronoun *this*, make sure that the **idea it refers to has been clearly stated**. For example, it is impossible to know exactly what *this* refers to in the following student writing:

• The tribe's traditional way of thinking was central to sustainable development, but they could not be successful without modern technology that makes development more productive. *This* is very important because the group established sustainability without changing their traditions.

The pronoun *this* might refer to the idea that "the traditional way of thinking was central" or the idea that "they could not be successful until . . ." or to an unstated idea that "the tribe did eventually use modern technology." If you cannot use the pronoun *this* with clear reference, state your idea another way.

Activities

1 **Notice in context:** Read the conversation and the paragraph from an academic text. Circle all instances of *this* and *that*.

1. Conversation: *After a job interview.*

JOHN: Well, I think he sounds qualified for what we're looking for. Especially since, you know, it's hard to find a good dedicated salesman that can travel all the time.

PAT: Yeah, that's right. And he says he can travel, and he's worked as a salesman before.

2. Academic writing: *From a handbook about film equipment.*

When selecting film equipment to buy for local projects, one should make sure that repair shops are of good quality and spare parts are quickly obtainable. If equipment has to be moved frequently between different locations, it must be able to withstand stress, so a strong carrying case is preferable. This seems obvious but is not always considered when selecting items.

2 **Analyze discourse:** Answer these questions about the conversation and paragraph in Activity 1.

1. In the conversation, underline the word *that* when it refers to an idea. State the idea below:

_____

2. In the paragraph, underline the word *this* when it refers to an idea. State the idea below:

_____

3 **Practice conversation:** Imagine you are at a party and overhear the following statements. Express your opinion of the statements using the type of phrase in parentheses.

1. MARY: I really wanted to go to the movies last night, but I was so tired. I went to bed at nine o'clock.

YOU: That's really too bad.
_____

(*that's* + adjective phrase)

2. STEVE: We didn't see you at the meeting yesterday. Someone said you left work early because you weren't feeling well and you might not even be coming to work at all today.

YOU: _____

(***that*** + wh- clause)

3. KATE: I'm not so sure, but Michael said that we would have to leave by five in the morning tomorrow to get to the airport on time.

YOU: _____

(***that's*** + adjective phrase)

4 **Practice conversation:** Think about something you recently read or heard about in the news. Work with a partner and take turns telling about the news story and commenting on it using as many of the patterns from the chart in Section B as you can.

EXAMPLE

A: This morning I read about a dog that saved a child in a swimming pool.

B: *That's great!*

A: Yeah, but I wondered why only the dog was in the yard with the child.

B: Yeah, *that's a good point.* . . .

5 **Practice writing:** Each paragraph below includes a sentence that begins with the pronoun *this*, but the idea that *this* refers to has not been clearly stated in the preceding sentence. Describe the problem and rewrite the passage to make it clear. If you cannot make the idea clear using the pronoun *this*, write the ideas another way.

EXAMPLE

Detailed records that report if an employee has done his/her job and handled difficult situations can assist in the evaluation process. ***This requires accuracy as well as consistency.***

Problem: *The pronoun **this** is unclear, because it could refer to unstated difficulties in keeping "detailed records," or to the process of "assisting in the evaluation process," or even to the employee doing the job well.*

Rewrite:
Detailed records that report if an employee has done his/her job and handled difficult situations can assist in the evaluation process. Keeping such detailed records requires accuracy as well as consistency.

1. The theory may come from a variety of sources: from experience or experiment, or from sudden insight. But wherever it comes from, the theory needs to be made clear. This is not to deny that teachers may be highly effective without following a theory.

_____
_____
_____

2. Some people will feel uneasy about the definition of "pedagogy" as "operational research," because it might cramp the teacher's style. This raises an issue which is important to the matters discussed in this book.

_____
_____
_____

He did a nice job
The Adjectives *Good* and *Nice*

What have you learned from your grammar textbook?

Adjectives are words that are used to **modify nouns**, giving extra information about them. They can be placed **(1) before a noun** or **(2) after a non-action verb** (*be, seem, sound,* etc.):

1. The *tall* **man** caught my eye.

2. That **computer is** *expensive*.

What does the corpus show?

A The adjectives *good* and *nice* are very **common** in **conversation**. They have an **imprecise, positive meaning**. (*See Unit 20 for more about imprecise words in conversation.*)

B **Four words** are commonly used to **modify *good* and *nice*** in conversation:

Modifier	Function	Example
really *real* *very*	making the adjective **stronger**	• Those are *really nice* pictures. • He was *real nice* though. • She's *very good* with children.
pretty	making the adjective **stronger OR weaker** (depends on context and intonation)	**stronger:** **A:** Bill's fifty-two. **B:** That's amazing . . . that's great. **A:** *Pretty good* shape for a fifty-two year old. **weaker:** • Grandma looks *pretty good*. She has shrunk, but she's probably not going to seem that much different.

C The expressions *not very good* and *not very nice* are also **common** in conversation, especially for **describing people** or **their behavior**. These expressions are **softer** than saying *not good* or *not nice*.

Regular Form	Softer Form
• This infopedia is *not nice* to use, but I will try.	• That's *not very nice* of him. [describing behavior]
• It's *not good* to use a strong shampoo.	• I'm *not very good* at this game.

D *Good* and *nice* are often used in **expressions** that have important **social purposes** in conversation. They are often in reaction to something the other person said or did.

Function	Typical Expressions	Example
1. **complimenting** on possessions, achievements	*That's a nice _____. You did a good / nice job*	• *That's a nice sweater.* Where did you get that? • *You did a real good job* on that test.
2. expressing **appreciation**	*how nice so nice*	• Well, thank you, Guy, *how nice* of you. • You're *so nice*.

Function	Typical Expressions	Example
3. expressing **approval** for an idea	*sounds good* *good idea*	**A:** Do you want chips and salsa? **B:** *Sounds good* to me. • That's a *good idea*, Mark. I like that.
4. giving **positive responses** in conversations that express interest and caring	*Good!* *Nice.* *That's good / nice.*	**A:** I found the wedding pictures. **B:** Oh *good!* **A:** How you feeling today? **B:** A little better than yesterday. **A:** *That's good.*
5. expressing formulaic **greetings** and **closings**	*have a nice / good day* *(weekend / evening)*	**A:** I'll talk to you Monday. **B:** OK, *have a good weekend*, Susan.

Note: Also see Unit 25 on the use of *good* instead of the adverb *well*.

Activities

1 **Notice in context:** Read the conversation. Underline *good* and *nice*. Look for examples of the four modifiers *(real, really, very,* and *pretty)* and circle the ones you find.

Two friends are discussing the weather and their recent vacations.

PAVLO: It's been such a long winter with the weather.

ANA: Yes, we need some sun.

PAVLO: I did have a break in the sun. I went to Puerto Rico for one week and that was nice. But other than that I've been here pretty much for the whole winter.

ANA: Yeah. I have too. I went to California for Christmas, and of course it's not very good for Christmas down there. It rains a lot of time. But it was nice to be there and, uh, I haven't been anywhere else since.

PAVLO: I have three cousins that moved to Florida.

ANA: Oh, nice. What part?

PAVLO: Um, De Monto, uh D something. It's on the Atlantic side.

ANA: Uh huh. Well, that's nice.

PAVLO: I haven't seen them for about twenty years, so I'm going to go down there right after the Easter break.

ANA: That's good, all the crowds will be gone. That's a good time to enjoy Florida. I really like Florida in the spring.

2 **Practice conversation:** Complete each conversation with the best ending from the box. Then practice the conversations with a partner.

1. AKIKO: You rode in an uncovered pickup?
   SAMI: Oh yeah.
   AKIKO: _____

   Why didn't he uh, take you in the front?
   SAMI: I just don't know.
   AKIKO: Unless he didn't trust you.

2. JOHN: I saw this cat with no home, and I went up to him and I brought him in the house.

   CARL: _____

3. *At the dinner table.*
   EVELYN: Hey, the eggplant is good!
   TOMÁS: Oh, glad you like it.
   EVELYN: _____

4. MOM: Kids, wake up. It's Friday.
   SON: _____

5. LIN: Where are you staying in Santa Fe?
   WAN: The LaFonda Hotel.
   LIN: _____

> **a.** And good job on the sweet potatoes.
> **b.** That's a nice place. It's right downtown.
> **c.** Her husband is a really good friend of mine.
> **d.** Oh, good. That's a good day.
> **e.** That's a pretty good guess.
> **f.** Well, that was a really nice thing for you to do.
> **g.** That's not very nice of him.

3 **Practice conversation:** First, go back to the conversation in Activity 1 and practice it with a partner. Then write a conversation between two friends. This conversation should include at least four different uses of **good** and **nice**. Use the suggestions in the box and also add your own ideas. Practice your conversation with a partner.

> • Greetings or closings
> • A question and answer about a mutual friend
> • Talking about vacation plans
> • A compliment
> • Expressing approval

A: _____
B: _____
A: _____
B: _____
A: _____
B: _____
A: _____
B: _____

Do this quick
Adjective and Adverb Choices

What have you learned from your grammar textbook?

Adjectives are words that are used to **modify nouns**, giving extra information about them. They occur before nouns and after linking verbs. **Adverbs** are used to **modify adjectives or verbs**. Many adverbs are formed by adding *–ly* to an adjective.

adjective adverb + adjective	verb + adverb

• The *empty* room was *very quiet*.   • We *walked quietly* into the room.

What does the corpus show?

A   In casual conversation, **adjective forms** are sometimes used to **modify verbs**. Speakers may omit the *–ly* that would make an adjective into an adverb. In addition, the adjective *good* is used by some people in place of the adverb *well*:

- You could do this *quick*.   [instead of *quickly*]
- Look at how *slow* this car is going.   [instead of *slowly*]
- I know you'll do *good* on the test.   [instead of *well*]

B   **Be careful!** In more formal speech and especially in informational writing (newspaper and academic writing), adjective forms are almost never used to modify verbs. Instead, **adverbs** are used:

- When air is inhaled into the lungs, evaporation occurs *quickly*. (ACAD.)
- The reactions would proceed very *slowly*. (ACAD.)
- Financial services stocks also did *well*, gaining 55.4%. (NEWS)

C   **Intensifiers** are modifiers that **strengthen the meaning of the adjective.** They are common in both conversation and writing. However, different intensifiers are used in conversation and informational writing. In conversation, the adjective *real* is common, as well as the adverb *really*. Only *very* is common in both conversation and writing.

	Most Common Intensifiers	Examples
1. conversation	*real* (an adjective form) *really* *very*	• I think I have a *real good* chance of getting in that school. • Those drinks are *really good* and they are *really cheap*. • This is *very interesting*.
2. informational writing	*highly* *extremely* *very*	• The evidence in the case is *highly ambiguous*. (NEWS) • When animals are kept together in large numbers, the effects of fright can be *extremely serious*. (ACAD.) • The proposal has a *very good* chance of passing. (NEWS)

Activities

1 Notice in context: First read the excerpts from casual conversations. Underline all adjectives used as adverbs and circle the intensifiers. Then read the excerpts from informational writing and underline the adverbs.

1. **Conversations:**

   a. IAN: I'm scared, I tell you. I don't even know where my classes are. I'll have to get a copy of my schedule and figure it out.

   AMY: Don't worry. You're going to do good.

   b. At school they always have that Santa's secret gift shop where the kids can do shopping for their family or whatever. This year one of my boys got me a little sewing kit for my purse. It's in a real nice hard plastic case.

   c. BILL: You know, that hotel chain is trying to buy the Santa Barbara Inn.

   JEFF: We went there once, and we never liked it at all.

   BILL: It's really expensive.

   JEFF: The service was really bad.

   d. *Telephone rings during conversation.*

   LIN: Excuse me. I'm gonna grab this phone real quick.

   DAN: Okay, no problem.

2. **Informational writing:**

   a. As long as the stock market continues to do well, gold will do poorly.

   b. Experiential learning methods ask nurses to experience something for themselves. The learning is personal and yet highly meaningful to the individual.

   c. Altogether, 1991 was a very good year for stocks.

   d. The former prisoner was extremely thin and managed only a weak smile for photographers.

   e. Minda wanted marriage and a child quickly because she's older, and she says her biological clock is ticking.

2 Analyze discourse: In the chart in Section C, *highly, extremely,* and *very* are listed as the most common adverbs that intensify the meaning of adjectives in informational writing. However, other intensifiers are common too. Follow these directions.

1. Get a copy of a recent newspaper. Find a sentence that uses *highly, extremely*, or *very* as an intensifier. Then find three sentences that use other adverbs that intensify the meanings of the adjectives that follow them.

   _____

   _____

   _____

2. Do the same with a book or an article on the Internet.

   _____

   _____

   _____

3 **Practice conversation and writing:** Complete each sentence with two adverbs (or adjective forms used as adverbs), one that you would most likely hear in casual conversation and another that you would most likely read in a newspaper.

EXAMPLE

The team didn't do ___real good / very well___ during the new coach's first season. They lost ten games.
(conv. / news)

1. It wasn't a _____ expensive helicopter. Only two people could sit in it.
(conv. / news)

2. The other committee members need this report as _____ as possible.
(conv. / news)

3. The bike is fixed now, and it rides _____.
(conv. / news)

4 **Practice writing:** In Activity 2, you found some new intensifiers in the newspaper, in a book, and on the Internet. Use three of these words in sentences of your own.

_____

_____

_____

_____

_____

_____

What have you learned from your grammar textbook?

Adverbs express many meanings (e.g., *carefully, now, here*). Adverbs can modify an adjective (***very** big*) or a verb (*She ran **quickly***). **Sentence adverbs** express an **opinion** about the entire sentence:

 • ***Fortunately,*** the car did not run out of gas.

What does the corpus show?

A **Amplifiers** and **downtoners** are **special adverbs** that **increase** or **reduce** the force of a statement. Each type has **three main functions**:

Amplifier Function	Example
1. **increasing** intensity 2. expressing **certainty** 3. showing **precision**	• I ***really*** want to go visit her. • Well, it's ***definitely*** not a kids' movie. • It's ***exactly*** twenty-five miles from my house to their house.
Downtoner Function	
1. **reducing** intensity 2. expressing some **doubt** 3. showing **imprecision**	• The dollar strengthened ***slightly*** against most major foreign currencies. • ***Maybe*** it needs water and oil in it. • He talked ***kind of*** like this.

B **Amplifiers and downtoners** are **more common in** conversation than in writing. But different amplifiers and downtoners are common in conversation and in academic writing:

	Common Amplifiers (* = very common)		Examples
1. conversation	***actually**** *too* *real* *very* ***really**** *of course*		• ***Actually,*** I talk to her a lot. • I'm gonna run to the store ***real*** quick. • That was ***really*** awful. • Her hair's ***too*** short. • ***Of course,*** I've read that.
2. academic writing	*certainly* *very* *indeed* *in fact* *more* *of course*		• Response strategies can ***indeed*** transfer. • The procedure provides a ***more*** sensitive measure. • ***In fact,*** the combination produced more rapid learning.

	Common Downtoners (* = very common)		Examples
1. conversation	*almost* ***probably**** ***like**** *a little* ***maybe**** *kind of* *pretty* *sort of*		• It's up to ***almost*** thirteen dollars a square foot now. • We'll probably be up here by ***like*** ten or something. • I'm getting ***pretty*** good at Jeopardy now. • It will ***probably*** be more effective.
2. academic writing	*perhaps* *probably* *possibly*		• Additional variation is likely at different times of the day and ***possibly*** in different locations.

C In **academic writing**, a **special kind of downtoner** shows that the information is a **generalization**, but that it is **not always true** or is somehow not absolutely true:

| approximately | mainly | often | roughly | somewhat | usually | for the most part |
| generally | nearly | relatively | slightly | typically | in most cases | |

- In the hilly parts of China the fertility of the soil is **generally** lower than on the plains.
- The subjects relied **mainly** on automatic detection.
- The professional player is **often** held to be socially inferior.
- These species are **typically** plants of the jungle formations.

Activities

1 **Notice in context:** Read the conversation and the paragraph from an academic text. Circle all amplifier and downtoner adverbs.

1. **Conversation:** *About a music group.*

   MARISSA: So, it's the three of you playing again tonight?

   JACOB: Actually, there's four of us. We have a bass player tonight, too.

   MARISSA: I was really impressed by Matt's guitar playing at the last concert.

   JACOB: Yeah, he's a real virtuoso. He's very talented.

2. **Academic writing:** *About students working for social change.*

   Early writers typically did not take students' efforts toward major social change in the twentieth century very seriously. Social scientists often found it easier to base their opinions about the motivations of their efforts on psychological explanations. They focused on the "alienation of youth," on the conflict between generations, and on the personal frustrations of young people. For the most part, students' protests and complaints were considered to be part of a new generation struggling for recognition, and therefore in need of striking out against their elders who were not giving them recognition.

2 **Analyze and edit:** Read this excerpt from a writing exam question about the importance of art in society. Decide if each boldfaced adverb is used appropriately for academic writing. If an adverb is used inappropriately, cross it out and write an appropriate substitute above it. If it is correct, write **C**.

Art may be defined as the creation or expression of something beautiful. ~~Really~~ *(Certainly)* art is a subject in which imagination and personal taste are more important for assessment than exact measurements or calculations. **Of course**, the importance of pieces of art, like paintings, movies, sculptures, or songs can **definitely** not be compared with the importance of scientific discoveries like Albert Einstein's theory of the universe. **Maybe** the value of art cannot be measured like gold or silver, but it can inspire people, entertain them or **sort of** make them think about cultural values and what is **real** important in life.

3 **Practice conversation:** With a partner, complete this script of a short commercial for a car. Use at least five more amplifiers and downtoners to point out important, interesting, and surprising information. When you are finished, practice the commercial with other classmates.

Scene: *A teenage girl and boy are listening to music in the boy's new car. They are on a date. The girl's mother is sitting in the middle of the backseat of the car, because she did not want her daughter to be alone on a date.*

BOY: *[To the girl, looking nervous]* I had a **really** good time tonight.

GIRL: Yeah, I did, too. I just **kind of** wish we had more privacy. *[Girl looks back at her mom]*

MOM: *[With her arms folded, looking upset]* **Actually**, I think you've probably had **too** much privacy tonight. This car isn't as small as it looks from the outside.

BOY: *[Suddenly looking excited, talking about his car]* _____

_____

GIRL: _____

_____

MOM: _____

_____

4 **Practice writing:** Reread the paragraph in Activity 1. Think of some social changes (women's equality, racial equality, democracy, etc.). What are motivations for young people to participate in social movements? Write a paragraph that responds to that question with examples to support your ideas. Use at least three amplifiers and downtowners (from Section C), and circle the adverbs as you write them. Compare your paragraph with a partner's.

Young people in the United States have been an important force behind many major social changes. I do not agree that their motivations are **mainly** based on a need to be recognized by their elders. I believe that many factors motivate them. For example, _____

_____

_____

_____

_____

_____

_____

Women are different from men
Adjective + Preposition

What have you learned from your grammar textbook?

Adjectives can occur either (1) **before a noun** or (2) **after a non-action verb** (*be, seem, become,* etc.):

    1. We have a **big cat**.

    2. My daughter **is sick** today.

What does the corpus show?

A When **adjectives** occur **before a noun**, they are almost **never followed by a preposition**. But **adjectives** occurring **after a non-action verb** can be **followed by a preposition**.

    • It brings back such **happy** thoughts.   • They **are happy with** the deal they got.

B In conversation, many **common adjectives** occur after a non-action verb **without a following preposition**. The adjectives usually **express a general comment** on a situation:

Adjective	Example
bad	• Well that's too **bad**.
funny	• That's not **funny**!
good	• I know the brakes aren't **good**.
great	• That's **great**!
nice	• That's really **nice**.
right	• I guess you're **right**.
true	• Yeah, that's **true**.

C Other **common adjectives** in conversation often take a **following preposition**. These adjectives usually occur with a particular preposition to make specific **combinations**:

Pattern	Adjective + Preposition Combinations		Examples
1. adj. + *of*	*afraid of* *aware of* *full of*	*sick of* *tired of*	• He's not **afraid of** my dogs. • I wasn't **aware of** that. • She's **sick of** living in the dorm. • I'm getting **tired of** his bad attitudes.
2. adj. + *for*	*good for* *great for*	*ready for*	• I think it's **good for** you. • These shoes are **great for** biking. • I'm not **ready for** winter.
3. adj. + *with*	*fine with* *happy with*	*wrong with*	• Well that's **fine with** me. • I'm **happy with** the deal I got. • What's **wrong with** you?
4. adj. + other preposition	*different from* *(different than)*	*mad at* *right about*	• Women are **different from** men. • Mom's **mad at** me. • You're **right about** that.

D In **academic writing**, most common adjectives after a non-action verb occur with a **following preposition** (or a following clause—see Unit 36). The **adjectives are different** from those used in conversation. They usually occur with a particular preposition and make specific **combinations** that are **common in academic writing**:

Pattern	Adjective + Preposition Combinations		Examples
1. adj. + *of*	*aware of* *capable of*	*independent of* *true of*	• The heat source should be ***capable of*** reaching at least 220°. • This pattern is ***true of*** all parts of the system.
2. adj. + *for*	*available for* *essential for*	*necessary for* *responsible for*	• There are several materials ***available for*** roofing. • The Dutch are ***responsible for*** introducing this system.
3. adj. + *in*	*common in*	*present in*	• Latent forms of energy are ***present in*** the fluid.
4. adj. + *for/in*	*important for* *important in*	*useful for* *useful in*	• A high flow rate is ***important for*** turbojet engines. • Many factors are ***important in*** determining the response.
5. adj. + *to*	*equal to* *identical to*	*similar to*	• It follows that this must be ***equal to*** the change in energy. • These results are ***similar to*** those reported previously.
6. adj. + other preposition	*consistent with* *dependent on*	*different from*	• This is ***consistent with*** previous research. • These areas are ***dependent on*** South Africa economically.

Activities

1 **Notice in context:** Read the two excerpts from conversations and the two paragraphs from academic texts. Circle the adjectives that follow non-action verbs. If the adjective is followed by a preposition, underline it. Do not circle possessives or numbers.

1. **Conversation:** *About someone's fear of cockroaches.*

   JULIA: It's weird because I am not afraid of snakes and I'm not really afraid of bugs, but for some reason knowing that there was a cockroach in that apartment . . . I couldn't stay there. Isn't that weird?

2. **Conversation:** *At a meeting about a company's budget.*

   CHAIR: So, if anyone is aware of any changes, let Carl know before Thursday of next week. Anything else? Are we ready for the vote?

3. **Academic writing:** *About researching levels of difficulty in reading programs.*

   Bjornsson's approach was different from that of many earlier researchers in two important ways: first, he set out to make his formula useful for making cross-cultural comparisons; and second, he chose not to use the students' language background as a factor in his studies.

4. **Academic writing:** *About methods of collecting data for social research.*

   There are several methods that are common in data collection, and they are personal interview, telephone interview, group response, direct observation, and mailed questionnaires.

2 Analyze and edit: Read these paragraphs written by English language learners. Underline each **adjective + preposition** combination and decide if each combination is written correctly. If it is correct, write *C* above it; if it is incorrect, cross it out and write the correct combination above it.

1. *From a writing exam question about changing lifestyles.* [Two combinations]

   Luxury goods are goods which make life pleasant but are not really necessary for everyday life. Our research gives information about the percentage of households with goods like cars and televisions in the years 1970 and 1980. As we found, the greatest increases can be found in heating systems and phones. Those luxury goods were not as common for 1970 as other goods; only a third of households had them.

2. *From a letter in a job application.* [Three combinations]

   I would like to apply for the job in your engineering firm that you advertised in *Presse* newspaper yesterday. My education and work experience are consistent in the job description in your ad. I am capable for working long hours, and I am available for an interview immediately.

3 Practice conversation: Debate the following topics with a partner. For each topic, choose one side of the argument and try to convince your partner that your point of view is the best one. Use each of the **adjective + preposition** combinations in the box at least once and any other combinations that you choose.

better for	*good for*	*happy with*	*right about*
different from	*great for*	*mad at*	*wrong with*

1. Driving a car versus riding a bike to work or school.
2. Reading the book versus watching the movie about the book.
3. Living in a city versus living in the country.
4. Sending a letter to a friend versus sending an email to a friend.

   EXAMPLE

   Riding your bike provides exercise, which is **good for** your health, and it is **better for** the environment than driving a car.

4 Practice writing: Choose one of the topics you debated above, and write a paragraph explaining your point of view. Use at least three **adjective + preposition** combinations in your paragraph. Share your paragraph with your partner.

   EXAMPLE

   I believe sending a letter can be **important for** communication between friends because it is more personal than an email. There are several other reasons, including . . .

_____

_____

_____

_____

_____

UNIT 28

It looks pretty awful though
Though and *Anyway*

What have you learned from your grammar textbook?

(1) The word *though* introduces an **adverb clause** that shows **contrast** or **unexpected result**.
(2) The conjunction *but* is used in **short responses** in conversation **to disagree** with another speaker.

    1. *Though* the weather is bad, we will have a picnic.

    2. —This apple does not look very good.
        —*But* this orange does.

What does the corpus show?

A   *Though* is NOT commonly used in conversation to introduce an adverb clause. But it is very **common in conversation as a transition** (a word that connects the ideas between sentences).

The word *anyway* is also **common in conversation as a transition**.

B   *Though* is used as a transition in conversation to show **contrast** or **disagreement** (like *however* in writing—*see Unit 29*). It has **three specific functions**:

Function	Example
1. expressing **contrast** with your **own previous statement**	**A:** There's no way those stains are ever going to come off, so for everyday use I guess that it's all right. It looks pretty awful *though*.
2. adding a **contrasting idea** to the **previous speaker's point** (without saying that the point is wrong)	**A:** That's just a garment bag, isn't it? **B:** Yeah. That bag is really expensive, *though*. [Speaker B agrees it is a garment bag, but adds a contrasting point.]
3. expressing **disagreement** with the **previous speaker's point**	[Watching a football game and discussing a penalty call:] **A:** Oh, that call's outrageous. **B:** That player did put his foot out *though*.

C   The transition *though* can be used like the conjunction *but* to show **contrast** or **disagreement**. However, these two words have **different positions** and **different impacts**.

Though vs. *But*	Example
though position: **end** of clause impact: sounds **softer** than *but*	**A:** Maybe he gave you the wrong herbs. You know, maybe he was a bad doctor. **B:** Those things were strong *though*.
but position: **beginning** of clause impact: sounds **stronger** than *though**	**A:** I used to make pasta, but it always got eaten right away. **B:** *But* you could make a bunch and dry it and store it dried or freeze it.

* Some speakers use *yeah but* as a very informal, less polite equivalent of *though*. It is less strong than *but* alone.
    A: You could take the truck.
    B: *Yeah but* my car is more comfortable.

D *Anyway* has **two common functions** in conversation:

Function	Position	Example
1. expressing **contrast** with the **previous speaker's point** (without saying that the point is wrong)	• usually at the **end** of the clause	**A:** I could cut some more meat. **B:** Oh, I don't know, I'm not sure that I want any more. **A:** I could cut it *anyway*.
2. signaling that you are **moving back to the main point** after a less important discussion or an interruption	• usually at the **beginning** of the clause • often occurs with *well, so,* or *but*	**A:** So you want me to come look at your classroom tomorrow, whether I go meet that—you got popsicles! [Discussion of popsicles for a minute.] **A:** *So, anyway*, want me to come to school tomorrow?

Activities

1 Notice in context: Read the conversations. Circle *though* and *anyway*.

1. *Family stories.*

FREDDIE: Do you remember Aunt Blanche now, Uncle Joe?

JOSEPH: I remember her.

FREDDIE: That would be Bousha's brother and his wife. Well, they had this daughter, Gloria . . . Remember Gloria? She was Dar's age. Anyway, she had a baby, but she never got married.

JOSEPH: Mm.

FREDDIE: Kathy, that's her little girl, she graduated this year, but Gloria's been dating this guy, but I think they were waiting for Kathy to graduate. Well, anyway, they got married this summer.

2. *Renting a car at the airport.*

CLERK: The Geo Metro station wagon - I think that would be your first choice.

ORLANDO: No, no, no, I'd rather spend more on the other car.

LETICIA: The other car isn't a wagon.

ORLANDO: I won't get into a Geo Metro. I don't feel safe. It's like a little two-seater . . .

LETICIA: Well, those Geo Metro hatchbacks aren't too bad, though. There'll be no room in the other car for our luggage.

3. *A mother talks to her adult children about relatives.*

SON: Well, Mom, do you have any other relatives?

MOTHER: I don't know whether dad's stepmother is alive yet. She couldn't be, though. No, she couldn't be alive because. . . . she might be, though. But I don't know where she lives or anything. I have to find out where she lives. So I don't know whether she's alive.

4. *Break time at work.*

JENNIFER: I'm gonna go have a cigarette. Would anyone like to come with me?

SANTOS: Smoky treats. It cuts like twenty years off your life or something.

JENNIFER: Well, who wants to live to be old, anyway?

2 **Analyze discourse:** Read the list of functions below. Then look back at Activity 1 and at the transitions you circled. What is the function of each transition? Above each one, write the appropriate letter from the list of functions.

    a. expressing contrast with your own previous statement

    b. expressing contrast with the previous speaker's point

    c. expressing disagreement with the previous speaker's point

    d. moving back to the main point after a less important discussion

3 **Practice conversation:** Practice the conversations in Activity 1 with one or two partners.

4 **Practice conversation:** Change these dialogues to be more conversational and softer in their disagreements. Cross out the sentences that are too formal. Rewrite them in the margin, using *though* or *anyway*. When you are finished, practice the dialogues with a partner.

  1. **A:** So how did she get you to buy the pots and pans?

      B: Well, she had to cook dinner for six in less than an hour.

      A: That, yeah, that sounds like an impossible job.

      B: However, she did it. She did it within forty minutes, from start to finish.

  2. **A:** They had the grossest food, like Lisa had a bowl of polenta.

      B: I like polenta.

      A: But this polenta was mushy. It was like eating soup, and then I had the ravioli, but it was like six raviolis with four pieces of spinach and it was weird, it was like . . .

      B: Are you serious?

      A: Yeah, and we still ended up spending like fifteen bucks . . . I ate the polenta.

  3. **A:** I'm thinking that when I graduate and you know, I'm a technical writer and stuff, I'm gonna want to get a nice laptop, just to have around, you know . . . carry the smaller one . . .

      B: But they're expensive. They're as expensive as a full size computer.

      A: Uh, actually they're more expensive.

Finally, on the negative side . . .
Transitions

Academic Writing

What have you learned from your grammar textbook?

Ideas in sentences can be connected with (**1**) **coordinating conjunctions** such as *and* and *but*, (**2**) **subordinating conjunctions** such as *although* and *because*, or (**3**) **transitions** (or "connectives") such as *therefore*.

1. It's raining today, **but** we will still have a picnic.
2. **Although** it's raining, we will still have a picnic.
3. It's raining. **Therefore**, the picnic is cancelled.

What does the corpus show?

A   **Transitions** are more common in academic writing than in other types of writing and conversation. The transitions express the **relationships between ideas**.

B   **Five functions of transitions** are **common** in academic writing. Although each function category includes many possible expressions, only a few are very common.

Function (in order of frequency)	Most Common Transitions (* = very common)	Example
1. expressing a **result**	*hence* ***then*** * ***therefore*** * ***thus*** *	• Obviously, ***then***, from what has been said above, it is always desirable to show the arrangement of the atoms in the molecule . . . • Evaluation looks at the relationship between teaching and learning; it ***therefore*** engages the participation of both teachers and learners.
2. giving an **example**	***for example*** * *for instance* *e.g.* (often in parenthetical statements or with phrases rather than sentences)	• Computers are most useful when task complexity is high and the decision-making is repetitive. ***For example***, airline reservation systems could not exist in their present form without computer support. • Several people (***e.g.***, Boden, 1978) have also argued that . . .
3. expressing a **contrast**	***however*** * *nevertheless* *on the other hand* *rather*	• The teacher did not give rules about the placement of adverbs. ***However***, if one of the students in class made a correct generalization, the teacher confirmed it.
4. **listing**, **adding**, or **concluding** points	*first* *finally* *in addition*	• A number of implications arise from the model that I have sketched out here. ***First***, the process is a scheme for research as well as teaching. • ***Finally***, on the negative side, it is natural to think in terms of additional steps that need to be taken.

(continued on next page)

Function (in order of frequency)	**Most Common Transitions** (* = very common)	**Examples**
5. **restating** an idea	*that is* *i.e.* (often in parenthetical statements or with phrases rather than sentences)	• The process of reviewing research and research findings will eventually lead you back to the same references. ***That is***, in time your readings will be quoting readings you have already encountered. • Seventy-eight percent of the learners reported noticing changes in their own pronunciation (***i.e.,*** they were becoming more Canadian-like).

C **Be careful!** Although transitions are very useful in academic writing and can make writing clearer, they distract readers if they are used *too* often. **Do NOT use transitions in every sentence.**

Activities

1 **Notice in context:** Read these two paragraphs from different academic texts. Circle the transitions.

1. *From a report on improving health.*

   It will take a complete re-education of the public before "health" regains its proper meaning. There seems little likelihood of more money becoming available. Therefore, improvements in health can be achieved only if existing money is put into policies that are more supportive of health. Such policies would aim, for example, to provide health education, eliminate poverty, create safety in the work place, and improve diet. Finally, these policies must ensure that everyone has the opportunity to enjoy these aspects of health.

2. *From a report on a training program for farmers.*

   The farmers' extremely small interest in learning through computer programs was perhaps predictable. A number said that they would find self-motivation and discipline difficult and would never see these forms of learning as substitutes for classroom training. On the other hand, the response to the use of video was astonishing. In all areas visited, video was acknowledged to be an extremely useful teaching aid, particularly for the more isolated farmers.

2 **Analyze discourse:** The following sentences contain transitions (or conjunctions) that are not listed in Section B, but they have the same functions. Can you find them? Circle each transition, and write its function on the line. Then find in Section B a transition that could replace the one you have circled and write it above the circled one.

1. Linguistics and psychology have made significant progress in recent decades, and, furthermore, both draw on centuries of careful thought and study. _____

2. An alien woman does not assume British citizenship automatically on marriage to a British citizen. Conversely, a woman who is a British citizen does not lose her citizenship if she marries a non-citizen.

   _____

3. Nationwide, there was only one full secondary farm school. Consequently, many farm children have never been to school. _____

4. Marx's and Engels's "general" stages often read like a generalized history of western Europe. But Eurocentrism seems much less excusable in the work of modern historians.

_____

3 **Practice writing:** This paragraph contains too many transitions. Cross out the transitions that decrease the effectiveness of the writing. Rewrite the paragraph on a separate piece of paper.

There are advantages and disadvantages to living in my hometown, Nantes. First, one advantage of living in Nantes lies in the possibility of using quick transport. For example, many buses are provided. As a bus comes every ten minutes to each bus stop, people don't lose their time waiting for a bus. Thus, these buses facilitate the lives of people living in Nantes. Second, Nantes also has many leisure facilities such as tennis and water sport activities, and also theatres and cinemas. For example, each of the six theatres offers at least six choices of different films. As a result, everyone can find a film that he/she likes.

4 **Practice writing:** The following sentences are related and appear in order, but they contain no transitions. Find three places where you could insert **(1)** a transition that expresses a result; **(2)** a transition that expresses a contrast; **(3)** a transition that precedes an example. Rewrite the sentences in paragraph form, including the three transitions, on a separate piece of paper.

- In many African nations before independence, mass education for black people, particularly beyond primary school, was not encouraged.
- While white settlers and colonial civil servants were provided with both government and private schools, many of them regarded education for the black population as politically dangerous.
- Educational structures were weak at independence, with very limited coverage above primary level for the majority of the population.
- Zimbabwe, achieving independence in the 1980s, faced leaner economic times than had Zambia in the 1960s.
- It embarked on an even larger program of educational expansion.
- After independence, the curriculum was altered by changing the content of some subjects—history and geography—and by introducing new subjects such as political education and sociology.

It would thus appear that . . .
Positions of Transitions

Academic Writing

What have you learned from your grammar textbook?

Transitions such as *therefore* have **several possible positions** in a sentence. (In contrast, conjunctions such as *and* must be placed between two clauses.)

- It's raining. *Therefore*, the picnic is cancelled.
- It's raining. The picnic is cancelled, *therefore*.
- It's raining. The picnic, *therefore*, is cancelled.

- It's raining, *and* the picnic is cancelled.

What does the corpus show?

A Although there are **several possible positions for transitions**, they are **not used equally** and they have **slightly different effects**. Individual writers often have different preferences for the placement of transitions, but the following general rules apply for the **most common positions** in academic writing.

Position (in order of frequency)	Description of Use	Examples
1. before the subject	• the most common position; this is the "usual" position • tells readers the relationship between two sentences before they read the second sentence	• The content of the test interacted with culture. *For example*, the content of a reading comprehension passage could be more relevant to one cultural group, relative to another. • Media need politics for their economic survival. *On the other hand*, politicians need to be known by the public; *hence*, they need media exposure in order to live their political lives.
2. immediately after the subject	• In this case, the subject is more important than the transition word, because the subject creates cohesion with the previous sentence. • often used when the subject of the second sentence provides a contrast with the first sentence • most common transition words in this position: *therefore*, *thus*, and *however*	• **In Portuguese**, the consonant clusters 'st,' 'sp,' and 'sk' occur, but only with a syllable division between them. **A Brazilian**, *therefore*, finds it difficult to pronounce 'st,' 'sp,' and 'sk' at the beginning of a word. • **At first sight**, it would seem that there are two possible results from the reaction. **Closer consideration**, *however*, reveals that this cannot be the case.
3. immediately after the verb *be*	• The subject (often a pronoun) refers to the same thing as the subject of the previous sentence. The subject comes first, to create cohesion. • also common with "expletive *there*" as subject • most common transition words in this position: *therefore*, *thus*, and *however*	• The ability to use **formulaic expressions** accounts for the fluency of the native speaker. **They are**, *therefore*, a crucial component of language competence. • Those who teach courses in English for Academic Legal Purposes (EALP) have often made use of law reports. **There are**, *however*, two major problems with the use of law reports in the EALP classroom.

Position (in order of frequency)	Description of Use	Examples
4. inside the verb phrase, OR **between** the main **verb and an object** that is a clause	• most common with "expletive *it*" as subject • other subjects usually refer to the same thing as the subject of the previous sentence • most common transition words in this position: **_therefore, thus,_** and **_however_**	• The major conclusion from these studies is that the library catalog works and users are skillful with it. **It would _thus_ appear** that low usage was not problematic. • The following picture emerges from the above discussion. **It should be noted, _however_, that all the points constitute assumptions**, supported by the literature to a greater or lesser extent.

B **Be careful!** It is **uncommon** for transitions to be placed **at the end of the sentence**, even when they are grammatical there.

- When a particularly close rapport develops between a human and an animal, such that the animal will follow its owner through the forest, the animal is called a batiti, "pet." One must still not talk to the pet in human language, **_however_**.

Activities

1 Notice in context: Read these excerpts from academic writing. Circle the transitions.

1. A wide range of personal preferences in children ages five to eleven made it impossible to serve an absolutely standardized breakfast. Most children, however, had breakfast cereal with milk, with the addition, or substitution, of buttered toast.

2. Teachers are likely to be required to engage in one-to-one dialogue with individual pupils as the basis for reviewing academic progress. Teachers are thus faced with increasingly divergent pressures.

3. It was found that young learners who study spoken Arabic mentioned that knowledge of Arabic contributes to achieving peace between Israel and its Arab neighbors. It seems, therefore, that the teaching of spoken Arabic in grades 4 to 6 helped to improve attitudes towards the other group, its language, culture, and speakers.

4. Today, most of us own machines which translate information from one form to another. For example, a tape recorder can translate sound into patterns of magnetization on a tape.

2 Analyze discourse: Look back at Activity 1 and at the transitions you circled. For each transition, tell its position and give one or more reasons why that position is effective.

1. Position: _____ Reason(s): _____
2. Position: _____ Reason(s): _____
3. Position: _____ Reason(s): _____
4. Position: _____ Reason(s): _____

3 **Practice writing:** Rewrite the second sentence in each pair to show its relationship to the first sentence by adding a transition. Choose from the most common transitions listed in Unit 29. Use each of the four most common positions in academic writing, deciding which sentence is best for each position. Be ready to explain your choices to a partner.

1. Helen's personality does not seem to have altered since her move into shared housing.
   Elizabeth has changed significantly.
   _____

2. Congress lacks power to regulate education directly, yet it does have the power to grant money to support education.
   By attaching conditions to its grants of money, Congress may regulate what it cannot directly control.
   _____

3. As defined in physics, a force can be exerted on an object and yet do no work.
   If you hold a heavy bag of groceries in your hands at rest, you do no work on it.
   _____

4. This teaching approach is based on the experiences and viewpoints of students rather than on an imposed culture.
   It is multicultural.
   _____

4 **Practice writing:** Follow these instructions to create sentences that use the indicated transition in an effective and appropriate way.

1. Write two sentences that have a contrasting meaning. Use **however** immediately after the subject.
   _____
   _____

2. Write two sentences, with the second sentence expressing a result of the first sentence. Use **thus** immediately after the verb **be** in the second sentence.
   _____
   _____

3. Write two sentences, with the second sentence expressing a result of the first sentence. Use an "expletive **it**" and **therefore** in the second sentence.
   _____
   _____

4. Write two sentences that have a related meaning. Introduce the second sentence with the appropriate transition of your choice.
   _____
   _____

What have you learned from your grammar textbook?

A **noun clause** can be the **object of a verb**. Noun clauses can **begin with the word** *that* **or a** *wh-***word.** The word *that* has no meaning in these clauses, and it is **often omitted**, especially in conversation.

        V   O

• I **think** (*that*) *he is sick today.*

        V   O

• I **wonder** *where* *you are.*

What does the corpus show?

A In conversation, **verb + noun clause** is commonly used to **express a lack of certainty about an idea.** The verb expresses the lack of certainty, and the noun clause expresses the idea. When ideas are certain, speakers usually state them as a simple sentence (without a verb + noun clause structure).

    LACK OF CERTAINTY: I **think** *the stores close at four.*
             CERTAIN: The stores close at four.

B The **most common "uncertainty" verbs** used with *that*-clauses have **literal meanings that refer to mental processes** (such as *thinking*), but they are used to **express different levels of doubt/certainty:**

Verb	Description of Use	Examples
think	• expresses **more certainty than doubt**, but exact level of certainty varies. Intonation and context often give clues to the level. • also used to express an **opinion.** *I think* or *I thought* can mean "in my opinion." • *I think you should* is often used to give **advice.** • extremely common in **present and past tenses**	• I **think** *the bowling fee includes the shoe rental too,* but I'm not sure. • I **thought** *it looked pretty cool.* [= In my opinion, it looked pretty cool.] • I **think** *you should* give this to Steven. [advice]
don't think	• *I don't think* X *is true* is the common way of expressing *I think* X *is **not** true.* • uses are similar to *think* (including **opinions** and **advice**) • extremely common in **present tense,** but past tense *didn't think* is **not common**	• I **don't think** *it will be a problem.* [= I think it will not be a problem.] • I **don't think** *you should* go there. [advice]
guess	• *guess* usually sounds **less certain** than *think* • often used to express an uncertain idea that is based on other **evidence in the context** • used almost exclusively as *I guess* • very **common in American English** but rare in British English	• I **guess** *you could say she was a poet.* • She tried to call me at like twelve last night. I **guess** *she was up packing late and she thinks that everybody stays up late.*
believe	• often used with same meanings as *think* but **less common** and **more formal-sounding** • *I can't believe* . . . is used to show **surprise.**	• I **believe** *this is your chair.* • I **can't believe** *you walked in there!* [laughing]

C In **conversation**, **most *that*-clauses** with verbs of uncertainty **omit *that*** (*see Unit 32 for more about omitting **that***).

D **Frequency information.** Expressions with ***I don't know* + *wh*-word clauses** are also extremely **common for expressing uncertainty**. In contrast, it is rare to use *I know* + *wh*-word clauses to express certainty.

Wh-Word	Example
what	• **I don't know *what*** you're talking about.
why	• **I don't know *why*** we're having so many problems.
where	• **I don't know *where*** she lives or anything.
how	• **I don't know *how*** that picture got in here.
whether	• **I don't know *whether*** the tickets came or not.
if	• **I don't know *if*** he'll like this.

Activities

1 **Notice in context:** Read the two conversations. Find all the verbs followed by noun clauses. Circle the verbs and underline the noun clauses.

1. *Picking colors at the paint store.*

CUSTOMER: I think it's a pretty color.

STORE CLERK: I believe your husband will be checking back with you.

CUSTOMER: Okay.

STORE CLERK: He came in the door and, uh, dropped that paint brush off. I guess he didn't have time to use it. I think he'll be calling you to check with you about the colors. That's the impression I got.

2. *At a family gathering, looking at photos.*

PAT: I can't believe I didn't bring my camera today. I thought I had it.

KAZEM: Oh, that photo's nice. Aren't the girls cute? I think you should frame it.

PAT: I didn't get Al. I don't know where Al was when I was taking these.

KAZEM: This was my grandfather. I don't know who this boy was, that wasn't me. This was my grandmother, my mother, and my oldest sister.

2 **Analyze discourse:** Look back at Activity 1 and at all the verbs followed by noun clauses you identified. Write the meaning of each one (***uncertainty, opinion, advice,*** or ***surprise***) in the margin. Draw an arrow between the structure and its meaning. Then answer the following questions about these sentences. Discuss the reasons for your choices with a partner.

1. Which ones express the most uncertainty?

_____

2. Which one is more formal than the others?

_____

3 **Practice conversation:** Work with a partner to develop a dialogue for each one of the situations listed below. Person A uses a variety of *I don't know* followed by *wh*-word clauses. Person B answers with sentences that include a variety of verbs followed by noun clauses. Practice your dialogues together.

1. Trying to cook dinner with someone.
2. Deciding where to put your new furniture.
3. Talking about where to go on vacation.
4. Discussing who to invite to a party.
5. A situation of your choice!

EXAMPLE

Getting lost while driving.

A: I **don't know where** that shopping mall is.
B: I **don't think** it's on this street. I **can't believe** we left home without a map!
A: I **don't know if** we can find it, now that it's getting dark.
B: I **think you should get off** at the next exit so we can ask someone for directions.

4 **Practice conversation:** Think about a topic that you have some questions or doubts about. It might involve a personal situation (for example, a job, choice of colleges, or where you are going to live) or a world condition (for example, global warming or world hunger). Make a few informal notes about your thoughts, opinions, and doubts. Use your notes as prompts to discuss the topic with a partner.

EXAMPLE

Notes for a discussion about getting a college degree:

Certain ideas/opinions:	need a degree for a good job
Less certain:	college expensive here
	4-year degree → more job options?
Uncertain/doubtful:	have enough money for college?
	maybe other students get loans — can I?
	less expensive college somewhere?

Sample opening for discussion:

A: I need a college degree for a good job, but I **think** it's really expensive here. I **don't think** I'll ever have enough money for tuition.
B: I **think** you could get a loan.
A: I **guess** a lot of students get loans, but . . .

I think I can find it
Deletion of *That* in Noun Clauses

What have you learned from your grammar textbook?

A **noun clause** can be the **object of a verb**. Noun clauses can **begin with the word** *that*, but it has no meaning and can be **omitted.**

- I **think** *that* he is sick today.   OR   • I **think** he is sick today.

What does the corpus show?

A Frequency information. **Omitting** *that* **vs. including** *that* in noun clauses that are objects of verbs:

- The great majority of noun clauses in conversation **omit** *that.*
- The majority of noun clauses in fiction **omit** *that,* but the proportion is not as great as in conversation.
- The majority of noun clauses in newspaper writing **include** *that,* but the proportion is not as great as in academic writing.
- The great majority of noun clauses in academic writing **include** *that.*

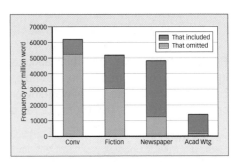

B **Three grammatical characteristics** are associated with the **omission of** *that*. These characteristics are very common in conversation. They are very rare in academic writing.

Characteristic	Examples
1. verb in main clause: *say* or **think**	• Dad **said** *the dog bit her or something.* (CONV.) • He also **thought** *Peter looked distinctly fatter.* (FICT.)
2. subject of *that*-clause: same as main clause	• I bet *I left the maps outside.* (CONV.) • **He** said *he felt disappointed by the president's actions.* (NEWS)
3. subject of *that*-clause: personal pronoun	• I knew *she was going to say that.* (CONV.) • Carrie thought *he was just being polite.* (FICT.)

The more of these characteristics a sentence has, the more likely it is to omit *that*. **Many noun clauses** in conversation exhibit **all three of the characteristics:**

- I **think** *I can find it.*

C *That* is usually **included** when the following **three characteristics occur:**

Characteristic	Examples
1. *that*-clause and *that*-clause	• She said *that* she saw the movie with him **and** *that* he hated it. (CONV.) • Adults all said *that* he was young **and** *that* soon he'd understand. (FICT.)
2. main clause passive verb	• LeRoy **was informed** *that* he was expected to drop Nate off. (FICT.)
3. noun phrase between main verb and *that*-clause	• I told **him** *that* you had to go to work. (CONV.) • He has explained **to me** *that* he doesn't believe in possessions. (FICT.)

Be careful! In newspaper writing and academic writing, even noun clauses that do NOT have these characteristics usually **include *that*.**

- In October, a jury had recommended ***that*** *the judge award the brothers $39 million.* (NEWS.)
- Gilligan discovered ***that*** *girls made more relationship-oriented statements than boys.* (ACAD.)

Activities

1 **Notice in context:** Read the three paragraphs from different types of writing. Underline the noun clauses where ***that*** has been deleted. Double underline the noun clauses which retain ***that***.

1. **Fiction writing:** *Diane is going to visit her grandmother, whom she has not seen for many years.*

   Golden clouds of flowers dotted the road. The sky was clear, the sun bright. But Diane couldn't enjoy the scenery. What would she say to her grandmother? She knew she was being silly; she had been told that the old lady wouldn't even know her. She might as well be a total stranger stopping by for a visit.

2. **Newspaper writing:** *A Mexican writer discusses his ethnic background.*

   I was a Mexican in California; I would no more have thought of myself as an Aztec than you might imagine yourself a Viking or a Bantu. Mrs. Ferrucci up the block used to call us "Spanish." We knew she intended to give us a compliment. We also thought she was ignorant.

3. **Fiction writing:** *The producers of a play want to know why the leading actor has disappeared.*

   After that, they went to see Mel, the director. He was tight-lipped and displeased and said he knew nothing of Bill's personal life. He also told them that he was unable to tell them whether or not Bill would be continuing with the show.

2 **Analyze discourse:** Look back at Activity 1. Work with a partner. Number each noun clause that you underlined or double underlined. For each noun clause, discuss why the choice was made to delete or not delete the word ***that***.

3 **Practice the structure:** Read the conversation. Cross out ***that*** introducing a noun clause when it would typically be deleted and underline ***that*** when it should remain. Discuss your reasons with a partner. Be careful – the word ***that*** also appears in other functions.

Three members of a teachers' association discuss how to strengthen the organization.

TONY: I think that classroom teachers can benefit from talking to people in higher education who have done research about effective teaching methods.

GAEL: Yeah, I really feel that we can benefit each other if researchers and teachers come together to talk. Sometimes that can lead to great problem-solving conversations about classroom issues.

VLAD: Well, I'll tell you that I've been asked to go down to speak to teacher education classes at Cameron University three times.

TONY: But do they know that the teachers' association exists and that they can come to us?

GAEL: Well, we had a conference. Do they come to the conference? No.

TONY: What I'm suggesting is that maybe we can form a committee to promote the conference.

GAEL: I think that a committee is good. At the conference we can promote membership.

VLAD: I think that we have a plan.

4 **Practice conversation:** Work with a partner. Complete this conversation about a day when one of you has missed class. Use noun clauses, and omit or include ***that*** appropriately. When you are finished, practice the conversation with your partner.

A: Can you tell me what happened in class yesterday? I was absent.

B: Well, Irina said _____ so Professor Fan worked on that for a while.

A: Did Fan tell _____?

B: He didn't mention a test, but he said _____

and _____.

A: Oh no. I think _____!

B: _____.

5 **Practice writing:** Imagine that you are submitting an article to a newspaper. Pick a topic that you know something about. Write a paragraph reporting what someone discovered, found, showed, suggested, and/or assumed. Choose ***that*** or ***that*** deletion.

EXAMPLE

Pets Help People at Senior Centers

Studies have shown **that** older people who have lost a loved one live longer if they have a chance to interact with animals on a regular basis. Dr. Leroy Plunger was told by nurses **that** patients' blood pressure went down after visits by dogs brought by family members. He said he saw the joy in his elderly patients' eyes as they petted and played with their beloved animals . . .

_____

_____

_____

_____

_____

_____

She seemed to like him a lot
Verb + Infinitive

What have you learned from your grammar textbook?

Some verbs can be followed by (**1**) **a gerund.** Other verbs can be followed by (**2**) **an infinitive,** or (**3**) **a noun phrase + infinitive.** Finally, some verbs can be followed by (**4**) either **a gerund or an infinitive.**

1. I *enjoy* **playing** soccer.
2. Sara *decided* **to play** badminton.
3. Sara *asked* Doug **to play** badminton.
4. Kate *likes* **playing/to play** tennis.

What does the corpus show?

A Overall, **verb + infinitive** combinations are **more common** than verb + gerund combinations. (*See Unit 34 for verb + gerund combinations.*)

B Although many verbs can be followed by an infinitive, with or without a noun phrase (NP), only a few verbs are very common with an infinitive. When we consider both conversation and writing, **the most common verbs fall into four categories of meaning:**

Meaning Category	Verb (+ Infinitive) (* = very common)	Example
1. want or **need**	*hope* ***like**** *need* ***want**** *want* NP *wish*	• Well, I *hope* **to see** you soon. (CONV.) • Wouldn't you *like* **to see** Aunt Irene? (CONV.) • I *needed* **to get** away. (CONV.) • I don't really *want* **to be** here. (CONV.) • We *want* you **to do** it. (CONV.) • Bobby did not *wish* **to hear** any more. (FICT.)
2. effort	***attempt**** ***fail**** *manage* ***try****	• American Express *had attempted* **to start** a similar promotion. (NEWS) • The information *failed* **to cheer** them up. (NEWS) • He *managed* **to communicate** to a certain extent through gestures. (ACAD.) • I *try* **to keep** my mouth shut. (CONV.)
3. begin or **continue**	***begin**** *continue* *start*	• The aircraft *began* **to lose** height. (ACAD.) • The movie theatre industry *will continue* **to thrive.** (NEWS) • She looked at him and *started* **to laugh.** (FICT.)
4. "seem" verbs	*appear* ***seem**** *tend*	• A lot of motorists *appeared* **to have joined** carpools. (NEWS) • Lisa *seemed* **to like** him a lot. (CONV.) • I *tend* **to sweat** heavily in warm climates. (FICT.)

Be careful! The verbs in the **"want** or **need"** category are very **common only in** conversation. They are rarely used in academic writing. The **other categories** are used in both conversation and writing.

C In **conversation**, **four** of the **verb + infinitive** combinations that were covered in Section B are **especially common**:

> • *want* + **infinitive** is extremely common. It is often pronounced as one word: "wanna."
> • *like, try,* and *seem* + **infinitive** are also very common.

D In **conversation**, *try and* is sometimes used as an **alternative** to *try to*. It is often used when the verb *try* is an infinitive:

> • We want to *try and* **find** a copy of that magazine. [= *We want to try to find a copy . . .*]
> • You don't have to *try and* **cook** everything in under ten minutes. [= *You don't have to try to cook . . .*]

E In **academic writing**, no single verb + infinitive combination is very common. In addition to the verbs in Section B, five other verbs are **relatively common**. They fall into **two meaning categories**:

Meaning Category	Verb (+ Infinitive)	Example
1. **report research findings**	*be found* (passive)	• Younger families *have been found* **to move** more frequently than older families.
2. **"allow" verbs**	*allow* NP *enable* NP *require* NP *be required* (passive)	• The size of the farm *did not allow* them **to make** a full-time living. • A checklist *will enable* you **to listen** to those words over and over again. • The test *required* participants **to identify** certain stimuli. • More work *is required* **to separate** molecules.

Activities

1 Notice in context: Read the conversation and the newspaper paragraph. Underline the **verb + infinitive** combinations.

1. **Conversation:** *Talking about Diana's four-year-old daughter, Amanda.*

   DIANA: I realized today that I nag Amanda too much. She takes forever for everything. Like getting dressed.

   JOAN: What do you say to her?

   DIANA: I just sort of try and bring her attention back to the task. But now I'm thinking to myself, I don't think I should say anything. 'Cause she knows what she needs to do.

   JOAN: She can put on her own clothes, right?

   DIANA: Yeah, but she's slow. I want to get ready to go out, and she'll start to get dressed, and then she'll get distracted and start playing, and I'll be like, okay, now you need to put your pants on.

2. **Newspaper writing:** *From an article about lead-based paint as a health hazard for children.*
   The primary source of lead exposure for children remains old, lead-based paint. Lead in paint made it more durable, but due to health concerns, manufacturers began to reduce lead as long ago as 1940. Lead in paint was finally banned in 1978. Doctors say children should be tested for lead poisoning first when they are about a year old, and then once or twice thereafter. If a child appears to have lead poisoning, it may be time to have the home checked as well.

2 **Analyze and edit:** Each of the following sentences has a **verb + infinitive** combination that is typical of conversation rather than writing. Change the verb or entire combination to one that is more typical of writing using the meaning category in parentheses. Cross out the original combination and write the new one above it.

1. Congressional Democrats have said they will sue the president if he ~~tries to~~ *attempts to* exert his veto powers. (**effort**)

2. Some employers will not want you to share your workload officially, but may be open to revising your job description to fit in with the company's needs. (**allow**)

3. In research studies, some people will not give personal information, or they don't even try and cooperate with the researchers. (**effort**)

4. In a study, Americans hoped to have the use of food stamps rather than policies for a guaranteed minimum income for all people. (**report research findings**)

5. For the first time last fall, all freshmen needed to take algebra. (**allow**)

6. Individual schools and determined teachers in the privacy of their own classrooms wanna violate numerous regulations and traditions. (**effort, with success**)

3 **Analyze discourse:** Read through **(1)** a newspaper article, **(2)** a page in a novel, and **(3)** a page in a textbook. List the **verb + infinitive** combinations you find in each reading. What meaning categories do they fall into? How do the verbs and categories differ among the newspaper, novel, and textbook? Share your findings with a partner.

4 **Practice conversation:** Write a conversation between two friends who want to study together after class. Use **verb + infinitive** combinations that are common in conversation. When you are finished, practice your conversation with a partner.

Scene: *A has a check to deposit at the bank and would enjoy eating an ice cream cone. B's mother asked her to go grocery shopping, and she also has nothing suitable to wear for her job interview tomorrow.*

A: So, what do you have to do before our study date?

B: I **need to do** some grocery shopping for my mom . . . _____

_____

_____

A: _____

_____

B: _____

_____

5 **Practice writing:** Below are sentences from three different types of writing. Create a paragraph for each one, including at least two **verb + infinitive** combinations most likely to appear in each type of writing. Write your paragraphs on a separate piece of paper.

1. **Newspaper writing:** Thick fog covered the city early today, cutting visibility during morning rush-hour traffic.

2. **Fiction writing:** My grandson was staring at me, and it occurred to me he was about to burst into tears or else run out of the room.

3. **Academic writing:** Scientists have found a way to help night shift workers get a decent day's sleep.

We couldn't stop laughing
Verb + Gerund

What have you learned from your grammar textbook?

Some verbs can be followed by (1) **a gerund**. A few verbs can be followed by (2) either **a gerund or an infinitive**.

 1. I *enjoy* **playing** soccer.
 2. Kate *likes* **playing/to play** tennis.

What does the corpus show?

A Although many verbs *can* be followed by a gerund, **only a few verbs are very common with gerunds**. Verb + infinitive combinations are much more common than verb + gerund combinations (*see Unit 33*).

B The **most common verbs** used with gerunds fall into **three categories of meaning**. These verbs are typical of conversation and fiction; they are rarely used in academic writing.

Meaning Category	Verb (+ Gerund) (* = very common)	Example
1. **begin, continue,** or **end**	*begin** get (NP)[1] *keep** keep on spend time *start** *stop**	• A dog *began* **barking**. (FICT.) • Let's *get* **going**. (CONV.) • The fear will *get* me **moving**. (CONV.) • She *keeps* **saying** she wants to go to Florida. (CONV.) • They've got stamina. They know how to *keep on* **going**. (FICT.) • I *spent* a lot of *time* **working** on my project. (CONV.) • Last night my leg *started* **hurting** in the middle of the night. (CONV.) • The leaves had not *stopped* **falling**. (FICT.)
2. **remember** or **think**	remember think about think of	• I *remember* **painting** with my dad. (CONV.) • Well, maybe I ought to *think about* **moving** here. (CONV.) • It makes me *think of* **being** sick. (CONV.)
3. **hear, see,** or other sense	hear NP *see* NP*	• They *heard* the door **opening**. (FICT.) • He could *see* Simon **looking** at him. (FICT.)

[1]Here ***get*** = to cause. See more on the meanings of ***get*** in Unit 4.

C In conversation, ***go*** + gerund is used with some **special meanings**. The most common are:

Meaning	Example
1. participating in a **recreational activity**	• We should *go* **swimming** before I take a shower.
2. expressing **dislike** or **surprise** at an activity	• I had to *go* **chasing** after them.
3. expressing **disapproval** (usually with "not")	• You *can't go* **yelling** at people.

D In **academic writing**, verb + gerund combinations are rare. **Only three verbs** are commonly followed by gerunds. They are useful when **describing a process** or **reporting research**.

Verb (+ Gerund)	Example
1. **be used for** (passive)	• Chlorine **is** widely **used for disinfecting** water.
2. **be achieved by** (passive)	• Communication can only **be achieved by relating** language with context.
3. **involve**	• Browsing **involves viewing** an ordered sequence of items.

E In most cases, when a verb can be followed by either **a gerund or an infinitive** and have roughly the same meaning, the **verb + infinitive** combination is **more common**. There is **one exception** to this pattern: the verb **start**.

In **conversation**, **start** + gerund is **more common** than *start* + infinitive:

MORE COMMON: They just **started** learning this song on Monday.
LESS COMMON: They just **started** to learn this song on Monday.

In **academic writing**, **start** + **infinitive** occurs more than *start* + gerund, but **neither combination is common**.

Activities

1 **Notice in context**: Read the conversation and the two paragraphs from different types of writing. Underline the **verb + gerund** combinations.

1. Conversation: *Two students discuss their future plans.*

YELENA: Once I get an academic degree I plan to become a teacher and that's what you do. You just stay in school. You continue to do what you always did. You stop getting degrees and you start earning a salary.

NADIA: That's one of the things I've considered, and then specifically I have thought about teaching English.

YELENA: It's a good field, and if you get some good students it's great.

NADIA: My sister has three degrees. And she just kept going to school. She never quit. She went to college for . . . I can't think of how many years she went to college.

2. Fiction writing: *Leaving a warm house at the wrong time.*

The first thing he realized when he got outside was that he had left his coat behind in the house. He began shivering. It was growing darker every minute, and he kept slipping into deep drifts of snow, and skidding on frozen puddles, and tripping over fallen tree-trunks, and sliding down steep banks, and scraping his shins against rocks, till he was wet and cold and bruised all over. The silence and the loneliness were dreadful.

3. Academic writing: *The relationship of computers and people.*

In discussing the development of computer systems, we shall examine some of the general questions that have arisen. This will involve reflecting a little on the nature of computers, the needs they fulfill, the side-effects they produce, and the psychology of human nature.

2 **Practice the structure:** Complete each sentence with a common verb from Sections B-E. Use the correct tense and form, and make sure the sentence makes sense. In some sentences, more than one answer is possible. The sentences from academic writing have been identified; the others are from conversation and fiction.

1. When we were driving back, suddenly his car _____started / began_____ making a weird noise.
2. I have _____ more time traveling in the east than I ever have in the west.
3. Hey, the blackout is over! They've _____ the street lights working again.
4. Ezinma lay shivering on a mat beside a huge fire that her mother had _____ burning all night.
5. I haven't seen you in such a long time. I _____ hearing you guys went to China, like for your honeymoon?
6. Go ahead, _____ walking. I'll catch up.
7. Meeting the basic needs of all citizens usually _____ focusing on a society's poorest members. (ACAD.)
8. We've got to move some of this furniture to make more space. We _____ about pulling the bookcase out of the baby's room and putting the toy chest back in.
9. How does garlic grow? I really have never _____ garlic growing.
10. One of his knees had been scraped. It _____ bleeding.
11. Make several copies of the outline. One copy should _____ for transcribing your notes. (ACAD.)
12. This is like the funniest picture. We couldn't _____ laughing when we saw that picture.

3 **Practice conversation:** Work with a partner. For each one of the topics listed below, tell your partner about a personal experience. Include the suggested **verb + gerund** combinations. For the last topic, supply your own **verb + gerund** combinations. Make sure you use the correct tenses and forms of the verbs.

1. Talk about a job you had or special project you did in the past.
   Use **begin, stop**, and **remember** with gerunds.
2. Think about a place that you like to go. Describe it to your partner.
   Use **see** and **hear** with noun phrases and gerunds.
3. Tell your partner about a childhood memory.
   Pick your own verb + gerund combinations!

EXAMPLE

Talk about your favorite recreational activity.
Use **go** and **spend time** with gerunds.

I like to **go jogging** in my neighborhood. I always go on the same streets so I can see how my neighbors' gardens are growing. When I'm not jogging, I **spend time gardening**, and I sometimes trade plants with my neighbors.

This is what happens
Be + Noun Clause

Academic Writing

What have you learned from your grammar textbook?

There are **two main types** of noun clause: ***wh*-clauses** and ***that*-clauses**:

- I don't know ***why*** he did that.
- I think ***that*** today is Thursday.

What does the corpus show?

A *Be* is the **most common verb** used with a noun clause in academic writing. The typical structure and uses of *be* + *wh*-clause are very different from *be* + *that*-clause.

B *Be* + *wh*-clause usually occurs with a **demonstrative pronoun as subject**. The pronoun refers to the previous sentence, while the *wh*-clause provides new information.

Wh-word	Function	Example
what *who*	providing further **explanation**	• The acts of weighing involve probing the box's interaction with gravitational field. **That is *what*** "weighing" is.
why	identifying the **reason**	• But no doubt these conclusions are open to challenge. **This is *why*** the issue needs to be evaluated for its classroom validity.
where	identifying a **place** or a **point in time**	• Robert Gravier was reported to have chartered the ill-fated Falcon Jet to take him to Acapulco. **Here is *where*** the intrigue started.
when	identifying the **time**	• As previously explained, **this is *when*** keyboard input is expected.

C The **subject of a *be* + *whether*-clause** is usually a **full noun phrase** that refers to a **question** or **issue**:

- **The question is *whether*** grammar ought to be taught as a separate formal subject.

D *Be* + *that*-clause usually has a **full noun phrase as subject**. In this case, the new information is in the *that*-clause, but the subject tells the reader **how to interpret the information**; e.g., an "explanation" or a "result."

- **One result was *that*** older people made greater head movements than younger people.

E **Frequency information.** Here is a list of **common subject nouns** in *be* + *that*-clause constructions:

Nouns (* = very common)		Examples
advantage	hypothesis	• Heath (1990) compares three studies on class differences in education, carried out respectively in 1949, 1972, and 1983. Very broadly, **his conclusion is *that*** class inequalities in education—at least for boys— have changed very little since the First World War.
answer	idea	• This points to a toxic effect of alcohol. **An alternative explanation is *that*** liver disease might be a major factor.
argument	implication	
assumption	interpretation	
conclusion	likelihood	• To explain such extreme velocities, we consider two possibilities. **The first is *that*** the masers are emitted from a molecular circle. **The second possibility is *that*** the masers are emitted from the nuclear region.
consideration	**point***	
danger	**possibility***	
difficulty	**problem***	
explanation*	**result***	• The night shift is supposed to be for working youth and adults. **The truth is *that*** many children also work.
fact	reason	
finding	truth	

Activities

1 **Notice in context:** Read the two passages from academic texts. Underline the noun clauses and circle the subject of each sentence with a noun clause.

1. *From a book about aquarium plants.*

    In the second year, these plants drop the underwater leaves and grow above the surface of the water. This is why this species is not suitable for an aquarium.

2. *From a study about primary school education.*

    One very valuable possible audience for project work might be younger children in the same school. Fourth-year students can produce booklets for first- or second-year students. A good test of suitability of the material they create is whether these younger children can read and understand it and find it enjoyable.

    The general point is that primary schools might be more imaginative and flexible in their staff assignments: there is no law that says that there should be one teacher to one class for all of the time.

2 **Analyze discourse:** Look back at Activity 1 and at the noun clauses that you underlined. Write the function of each noun clause (***explanation, reason, time, information, question/issue***) in the margin. Draw an arrow between the noun clause and its function. Discuss with a partner.

3 **Practice the structure:** Complete each sentence with a word from the box. Look at Sections B-E for examples of typical patterns.

point	*that*	*whether*	*who*	*where*	*when*	*why*	*result*

1. The interesting question for political sociology is _____*who*_____ controls or dominates the society.

2. The _____ is that, when reading a text for research, students are unlikely to find answers to their research questions in just one area of the text, so students are forced to be selective in what they read. This is _____ the skills of skimming a text to gain a general impression are very useful.

3. One particular time when we are concerned with several computer structures is _____ we transfer programs from an old computer to a new one.

4. A much more complicated question is _____ it might be necessary to consider international law as the default law even for local contracts that do not expressly contain those laws covered by international guidelines.

5. Teacher-training, which still follows traditional teaching techniques, does not offer teachers sufficient guidance for them to be able to adapt to the new requirements of the curriculum, and the _____ is that pupils are inadequately guided, and projects and assignments are poorly executed.

6. The fact is _____ the family is so important in most people's social structure and in personal life that much social work cannot be carried out with the client unless it is within the family context.

4 **Practice writing:** Read the first paragraph from a news article. Using the information in the paragraph and your own ideas, write a paragraph to predict how the story ends, and explain your prediction. Include at least one of each of the following types of combinations in your paragraph: *be + **whether**, be + **wh-**word, be + **that***.

Lachina, then 16 years old, was carrying her cousin Pam on her shoulders in the swift moving waters of the Kaweah River. Lachina slipped on the rocky bottom of the river, and her hair caught in the buttons of Pam's swimsuit as Lachina's head went underwater. They began thrashing. "All of a sudden I felt this pushing," Lachina said. "A lion shoved us — two panicking girls — from behind toward shallow water."

EXAMPLE
The main question now **is whether** the lion will help or hurt the two girls. One possibility **is that** the lion did not realize the girls were humans. It might. . . .

_____ _____
_____
_____
_____
_____

It is possible that . . .
That-Clauses or Infinitive Phrases for Attitudes

Academic Writing

What have you learned from your grammar textbook?

The grammatical word *it* can occur as the **subject** of a sentence when **a *that*-clause** or **an infinitive phrase** comes at the end of the sentence:

- **It** is clear ***that*** *you did not study.*
- **It** is hard ***to work*** *at night.*

What does the corpus show?

A *That*-clauses or infinitive phrases with *it* as subject are **common** in academic writing, but rare in conversation. These structures are some of the most important ways to **express attitudes** in writing.

B *It* + *is* + **adjective** + *that*-clause. This structure is used to **evaluate an idea**. The adjective expresses the author's attitude or evaluation, and the idea is expressed in the *that*-clause.

Evaluation	Adjectives		Examples
1. certainty	*certain* *clear* *evident*	*obvious* *plain* *true*	• It is **clear *that*** *they will not be identical.* • It is **obvious *that*** *good interview schedules are important tools.* • It is **true *that*** *change is not always linear.*
2. possibility	*likely* *possible*	*probable*	• It is **likely *that*** *we are dealing with a generation effect.* • It is **possible *that*** *this was a confounding variable.*
3. doubt	*doubtful*	*unlikely*	• It is **unlikely *that*** *the result would provide an accurate comparison.*
4. importance	*crucial* *essential*	*imperative* *important*	• It is **essential *that*** *the child spells accurately.* • It is **important *that*** *the body should move as a harmonious whole.*
5. other attitudes	*amazing* *arguable* *inevitable*	*interesting* *noteworthy* *surprising*	• It is **arguable *that*** *this interest has intensified recently.* • It is **interesting *that*** *the short-eared owls have the lowest percentage of bone preservation.*

C *It* + *is* + **adjective** + **infinitive phrase**. This structure is used to **evaluate an action**. The adjective expresses the author's attitude or evaluation, and the action is described in the infinitive phrase.

Evaluation	Adjectives		Examples
1. possibility	*possible*	*impossible*	• It is **possible *to compare*** *the effects of the two experimental conditions.*
2. difficulty	*difficult* *easy*	*easier* *hard*	• It is **difficult *to define*** *the terms "reactive" and "unreactive."* • It is **easy *to see*** *why this should be so.*
3. importance	*essential* *important*	*necessary* *vital*	• It is **essential *to document*** *that the procedures are actually carried out.* • It is **necessary *to specify*** *the names of all functions.*
4. other attitudes	*advisable* *best* *convenient* *desirable*	*helpful* *interesting* *reasonable* *useful*	• It is **convenient *to discuss*** *these processes in two parts.* • It is **reasonable *to expect*** *that public attitudes about attempted suicide will affect its incidence.*

D **Noun +** *that***-clause.** This structure is also commonly used in academic writing to **evaluate an idea**. In this case, the noun expresses the author's attitude or evaluation, and the idea is expressed in the *that*-clause.

Evaluation	Nouns	Examples
1. certainty	*conclusion* *fact* *little doubt* *no doubt*	• The **fact** *that* the "adornment" theory was entertained for so long deserves some explanation. • There is **no doubt** *that* our conceptions of conscious episodes do indeed include relational components.
2. possibility	*assumption* *belief* *claim* *possibility* *suggestion*	• This book is written in the **belief** *that* contemporary social theory stands in need of a radical revision. • There is a **possibility** *that* some sediment could get into the milk.

Activities

1 **Notice in context:** Read the two passages from different academic texts. Underline the *that*-clauses and infinitive phrases. Circle the evaluative nouns and adjectives that are modified by those clauses and phrases.

   1. *From a study about discrimination against women in two large companies.*

     It is hard to know how to measure this kind of evidence. It is not at all unlikely that some pressure was put on women in these two key firms, but it may have been more persuasion rather than intimidation.

   2. *From a handbook about conditions for farming.*

     While there appears to be conflict of opinion regarding the best temperature of the water, there is little doubt that in some regions the water may become excessively hot. Investigations indicate that high water temperature adversely affects grain development.

2 **Analyze discourse:** Look back at Activity 1 and at each noun or adjective that you circled. Write the type of evaluation that it gives (*certainty, possibility, doubt, difficulty* etc.) in the margin. Draw an arrow between the noun/adjective and the evaluation type. Discuss with a partner.

3 **Practice the structure:** Complete each sentence with an appropriate noun or adjective, plus *that* or *to*, from the lists in Sections B-D. There may be more than one possible answer.

   1. If there is concern about whether there is a sufficient amount of time for the analysis of data, it may be _____ consult with others regarding realistic periods of time for the completion of research.

   2. Should parents teach children good manners and even good beliefs? There is no _____ children learn far more by example than by instruction, and for that reason teachers have a continuous obligation to behave well themselves.

   3. Once the beer can had been invented, it was _____ it would eventually take the place of the bottle all over the world.

(continued on next page)

4. Given that science is often thought of as a laboratory-based activity, rather than a "bookish" subject, it is _____ note that in three of the four schools studied, science departments had begun activities to develop basic library and information retrieval skills as part of the curriculum.

5. From discussions with younger students, it was _____ for many young people the image of the bookstore was old fashioned, dusty, a place for scholarly introverted people. Yet many of the children had been in bookstores and knew them not to be so.

4 Practice writing: Express your opinion on each one of the topics listed below. Use *It + is + adjective +* *that*-clause or **infinitive phrase** for each topic.

1. Learning to play an instrument at an old age
2. Writing a best-selling novel
3. Speaking more than one language
4. Traveling to foreign countries

> **EXAMPLE**
> Training a dog to deliver the newspaper to its owner
> It is **difficult to train** a dog to deliver the newspaper.
> It is **likely that** the dog will chew up the newspaper before delivering it.

_____
_____
_____
_____
_____
_____

5 Practice writing: Look back at Activity 4. Choose one of the topics and write a paragraph that explains your opinion in more detail. Include at least two more *that*-clauses and infinitive phrases to express your evaluations.

> **EXAMPLE**
> The **assumption that** a dog can be trained to do anything is **unlikely to be** true. For example, it is **difficult to train** a dog to deliver the newspaper. Unless the dog is very obedient, it is **likely that** it will chew up the newspaper before delivering it . . . .

_____
_____
_____
_____
_____

. . . and she goes oh don't worry
Reporting What Someone Said

What have you learned from your grammar textbook?

There are two ways to report what someone said: (**1**) **Direct speech** quotes the exact words of the speaker, often introducing them with the "quoting verbs" *said* or *asked*. (**2**) **Indirect speech** does not use the exact words of the speaker. It uses a reporting verb and an indirect statement (or "noun clause").

    1. Ali **said**, "*I **plan** to go to the party*."   **2.** Ali **said** *he **planned** to go to the party*.

What does the corpus show?

A In real conversations, **direct speech** is **rarely an exact quote** of previous speech. The direct speech may reword the idea, provide a summary, or even express the speaker's thoughts more than exact speech.

    • I called and **said** *I'm ready to move into the apartment,* and they **said** *oh, sorry we already sublet—we already leased it.* And I **said** *excuse me, I've been calling you from Utah all summer long.*

B *Say* is **commonly used** in **direct speech** in conversation. *Ask* is rarely used (but *ask* is common for indirect speech). **Three other expressions** have become popular recently.

Verb/ Expression	Description of Use	Examples
1. *say*	• most common verb	• And so I **said** *what are you doing?*
2. *go*	• most often in simple present tense • used among friends • very informal • most common with younger adults but widely used	• He **goes** *I don't like to see girls in tight jeans.* • Jill said Annette called and Paul **goes** *well I didn't get the message.*
3. *be like*	• can be used for thoughts (rather than speech) • used among friends • very informal • most commonly used by teenagers and young adults; also used by many older adults	• I'm **like** *are you from Idaho City* and she's **like** *no do I look like it?* • Amy **was like** *uh, I think we should just buy some shelves.* • I spun around a couple of times, ran into a ditch and I'm **like** *what the heck just happened?* [describing a car accident]
4. *be all*	• can be used for thoughts (rather than speech) • used among friends • very informal • most common among teenagers and young adults; rarely used by older adults	• He's like *well you know we always have a hard time finding a third person to go with us,* I'm **all** *hey I'm willing.* • He **was all** *I love you sweetie.*

C The **discourse markers** *well, oh, look,* and *okay* are sometimes used to mark the **beginning** of **direct speech**. (*See Unit 48 for more on discourse markers.*)

    • And I said ***well*** *I'm gonna put it in, put a little five dollars in the thing and send it to the little children.*
    • They brought the car over here and I said ***oh,*** *you made it over here with it.*
    • He said ***look,*** *you guys have got to get together as a team and make a decision.*

D **Direct speech** makes a story sound more **immediate and exciting** for the audience. Adding to that effect, many speakers use **"historic present" for the quoting verb**. This means that **present tense** is used to **refer to past time**.

- She was sitting there eating the rest of this cheesecake, and she **SAYS** *what is this?* It **was** a fingernail.
- Mom **went** on this wine shopping spree and she **bought** these bottles when she **was** here, and she **GOES** *oh don't worry, well I just wanted to help you guys get a wine rack going.*

Be careful! It is **difficult to use** the informal quoting verbs and "historic present" tense appropriately. In fact, you **do not need to produce** those forms at all. However, it is **important to be able to understand** when native speakers use them!

Activities

1 **Notice in context:** Read these examples of reporting speech in conversation. Circle the words that introduce direct speech.

1. *Reporting on a conversation with the doctor about diet.*

   He said to me the last time I was there, he says okay, well, you know what, let's add back two supplements. I go supplements? Pills? That's what you wanna add back, is just those pills? He goes wait, wait, wait. Okay, okay. I say how about a grain, you know. He goes okay corn tortillas. I said corn tortillas. You mean just the corn tortillas? How about corn bread, corn muffins? He's like no, no, no, just corn tortillas.

2. *Reporting on a conversation with an angry boyfriend.*

   He, he walked out, and Jason and Theresa were laughing at me, and he's all thanks a lot, he goes that was rude, and I go darn, you know I was just kidding, and I said and so do they. He goes fine.

3. *Reporting on Mom at the movies.*

   STAN: My mom saw *Ace Ventura*.
   SULIM: Oh no.
   STAN: She's all I just saw *Pet Detective*. I'm all that's *Ace Ventura*, Mom.

2 **Analyze discourse:** Read Jennifer's reporting on a conversation with her colleague Suzi. Circle *go* and *be like* when they introduce direct speech and underline the direct speech.

1. Suzi asked me if I was gonna go to the seminar on Friday. She goes well, Jennifer, are you gonna go?
2. I go there won't be anyone there. She says well, Ken will be there.
3. I go he's teaching class from like eight thirty to noon.
4. She's like well, the seminar's for everybody.
5. I go oh, so the whole campus can close and everybody will go?
6. She's like well, yeah.

3 **Practice conversation:** Read what your friend Kevin says. Then check (√) any response that is appropriate (there may be more than one possible response).

1. KEVIN: It was that night a couple weeks ago when they had all those sales. So my wife goes out to buy me a watch, and I'm all I'd like a Rolex*.

_____ **a.** Why did she say that?
_____ **b.** She's shopping right now?
_____ **c.** Did she laugh when you told her that?
_____ **d.** Does she always announce when she's leaving?

2. KEVIN: I couldn't find my watch for a week, and my friend's sitting in our living room, and suddenly he goes oh, here's your watch.

_____ **a.** Where the heck did he find it?
_____ **b.** I don't see him in the living room now.
_____ **c.** Why did he leave?
_____ **d.** Did he give it to you before he went out?

3. KEVIN: I asked the professor what time class gets out and he was all eight or eight-thirty, isn't it on the syllabus?

_____ **a.** I wonder why he didn't answer you.
_____ **b.** The teacher doesn't know when his class ends?
_____ **c.** Did he do it all nine times too?
_____ **d.** Maybe he was busy grading papers.

4. KEVIN: I asked the professor what time class gets out, and he was all involved in checking papers, and he completely ignored me.

_____ **a.** He never even looked up?
_____ **b.** He's such a nice guy. I wonder if he heard you.
_____ **c.** Teachers always tell students things they DON'T need to know.
_____ **d.** He had the time to tell you he was involved with papers, but he couldn't say when class gets out?

---
* A Rolex is a very expensive watch.

The authors argue that . . .
Reporting What Someone Wrote

What have you learned from your grammar textbook?

You can report what someone said by using a **reporting verb and noun clause** (an "indirect statement").

- John **said** *that the show began at eight o'clock.*

What does the corpus show?

A In academic writing, it is more common to **report what someone wrote** rather than what someone said. Usually **general ideas** or the **overall findings** of a study are reported, rather than a single statement.

B There are **three grammatical patterns** that are often used for **reporting what someone wrote**:

Grammatical Pattern	Examples
1. **reporting verb + *that* noun clause** (most common)	• The authors **argue *that*** monitoring is a crucial feature of interaction. • Noels (1994) **demonstrated *that*** self-confidence also plays a role.
2. **reporting verb + noun phrase** as direct object	• Foley & Wallace (1974) **describe** many of the desirable characteristics.
3. ***as* + subject + reporting verb**	• It may indeed be the case, **as Izumi (2003) contended**, that attention and reflection are linked. • **As Stocking has shown**, an innovation may be effective but not adopted widely.

C The **reporting verbs** in academic writing often indicate **how certain** the information is. Of course, the specific meanings of verbs are also important; for example, *find* is different than *describe* even though both have high levels of certainty.

Certainty Level	Reporting Verbs (* = most common)			Examples
1. very certain	*conclude* *demonstrate* *describe* *explain*	***find*** *note* *present* *prove*	*report* ***show**** *state*	• As Burawoy **notes**, *this is not surprising . . .* • The publications **show** that efficient production is not confined to large farms.
2. less certain	*argue* *claim* *contend* *hypothesize*	*imply* *indicate* *maintain*	*postulate* *propose* ***suggest****	• Some **have implied** that virtually no constraints exist (e.g., Thomason 1988). • Mallier and Rosser **have** also **suggested** that changes in laws made it easier to recruit part-time workers.

Be careful! The same verbs can also be used for reporting new information. For example, ***suggest*** is often used to report the findings of a new study (*see Unit 10*).

D A number of **considerations** affect the **tense** that is **used for reporting verbs.** Sometimes editors or journals have specific policies about what tense to use. Other considerations include the following:

Consideration	Tense of Reporting Verb	Examples
1. reporting ideas that **continue to be true** or that you **support**	• **simple present** or **present perfect** • simple present also typical in the noun clause	• Unger (1983) and Henley (1985) **suggest** *that feminist psychology **is** interdisciplinary by nature.*
2. reporting studies with **conflicting** findings or ideas that you want to **argue against**	• **simple past**	• Qi's (1998) study **identified** *the factors that influence behaviors.* . . . On the other hand, a more comprehensive study (Woodall, 2000) **reported** *that . . .*
3. **summarizing** what has been **written by many people**	• **present perfect** • often followed by sentences about individual writers	• Several researchers **have argued** *for a distinction between awareness and learning. For example, Tomlin and Villa proposed . . .*

Activities

1 Notice in context: Read these examples of academic writing. Circle the verbs that report what someone wrote.

1. *Attitudes toward laws and breaking the law.*

   In their study of civic activity in 1959, Almond and Verba repeatedly noted that, in all five countries that they studied, the better educated people were more likely to participate in the political process and to believe that they could do something to change laws which they felt were unjust.

2. *Neighborhood networks of friendship and support.*

   Lee has also proposed a classification of neighborhoods, including the social acquaintance neighborhood, a small area in which people "keep themselves to themselves" and where the main support in times of trouble is from relatives rather than neighbors.

2 Analyze discourse: Read each pair of statements. Circle the letter of the statement that shows the greatest level of certainty.

1. **a.** Singleman and Tienda (1985) show that manufacturing industries declined from 36.7% to 30.7%.
   b. Conway (1958) suggested a Universal Computer-Oriented Language or UNCOL.

2. **a.** Levi-Strauss (1969) proposed that, since women are the most important resource that men have, a system for exchanging women always underlies the social control of marriage.
   b. As Berg (1981) finds, women's explanations of their success are more modest when they know they will be made public, and also when a friend has failed at the same task.

3. **a.** A key part of Mitev's paper explains advances in library catalogue design.
   b. Habermas and Offe claim that advanced capitalism cannot be understood solely in terms of the relation between capital and wage-labor.

3 **Practice the structure:** Read the notes taken by a student about an article about teaching English as a Second Language. Then complete the sentences. Describe the study and levels of certainty appropriately.

> R. Red: 1975 study analyzed proficiency exams (oral and written)
> findings = learners who studied grammar the most scored highest
> Red thought that ESL could focus only on grammar rules and still develop conv. & writing skills.
> much contradictory evidence – e.g., Pink's 1997 study = variety of practice is most effective

1. _____ that learners who studied grammar intensively scored higher on proficiency tests.

2. In the 1970s, many teachers believed, as _____, that studying grammar develops students' spoken and written proficiency.

3. However, _____ very different results, with a variety of practice being most effective.

4 **Practice writing:** Use the notes about Red's study and the notes below to write a paragraph about research on teaching English as a Second Language. Use appropriate grammatical patterns, reporting verbs, and tenses. You can also include your own thoughts. Share your writing with others, and be prepared to explain your choices.

> G. Green: 1983 essay said that the need for communication should be the first goal in ESL teaching
> Green believed: grammar accuracy follows from learning how to talk
> evidence = observing young children learning their first language. No ESL study.
>
> B. Brown: 1990 classroom experiments using materials from everyday life
> In his classroom, conv. and writing practice based on real student communication problems
> "authentic materials" students scored higher on tests than students from traditional class
>
> P. Pink: 1997 study – compared many teaching methods
> classes using variety of techniques, including but not only grammar practice – most effective

Teaching English as a Second Language: A Research Paragraph

Red (1975) **argued** that grammar is the most important thing for second language students to learn, but Green. . . . _____

_____

_____

_____

_____

_____

Evidence for life on Mars
Modifiers in Noun Phrases

Informational Writing

What have you learned from your grammar textbook?

There are several different kinds of modifiers that can occur in a noun phrase. **Adjectives, participles**, and **nouns** as modifiers occur **before** the head noun:

- *beautiful* flowers
- *interesting* story
- *vegetable* soup

Adjective clauses, adjective phrases, and **prepositional phrases** occur **after** the head noun:

- a friend *who lives next door*
- the girl *sitting over there*
- the lamp *on the table*

What does the corpus show?

A In informational writing (newspaper and academic writing), over half of all **noun phrases include a modifier**. But in conversation, most noun phrases consist of only a single noun or pronoun.

B In writing, **modifiers before** the head noun and **after** the head noun are about **equally common**. Many noun phrases have both:

- the *educational* goals *which they set for disabled pupils*
- a *new wake-up* service *that eliminates rude alarm clock awakenings*

C Frequency information. **Adjectives** and **nouns** are **common BEFORE the head noun** in writing, but **participles** are relatively **rare**.

Modifier BEFORE Head Noun	Frequency	Examples	
1. adjective	very frequent	• a *great* success	• the *important* question
2. noun	very frequent	• *food* prices	• *health* insurance
3. *-ing* participle	NOT frequent	• *flashing* lights	• an *exciting* discovery
4. *-ed* participle	NOT frequent	• *exhausted* survivors	• *complicated* instructions

D Frequency information. There are four **main types of modifier** that occur **AFTER the head noun** in writing.

Modifier AFTER Head Noun	Frequency	Examples
1. **prepositional phrase** as an adjective phrase	extremely frequent	• evidence *for the association of virus particles with the pancreatic cells of the chick*
2. **adjective clause***	relatively frequent	• laborers *who live in the towns where they work*
3. **adjective phrase*** *-ing* phrase *-ed* phrase infinitive	less frequent	• activities *involving the close use of vision* • categories *based on medical criteria* • the person *to see*
4. **appositive noun phrase**	less frequent	• Browning, *the Episcopal bishop*

*See Units 41–43, and 47.
**See Units 44 and 45.

E **Prepositional phrases** are by far the **most common type of modifier** in academic writing. They often occur together in a series. Usually, these prepositions do not have their literal "physical" meaning (*see Unit 46*):

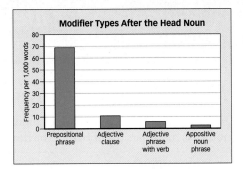

- Certain characteristics of matrices are of particular importance *in dynamical studies of systems.*
- The College of Pharmacy has gathered information *from world literature on the chemistry of 70,000 plants.*

Activities

1 **Notice in context:** Read the two paragraphs from different academic texts. Circle the head nouns and underline each noun modifier.

1. *The history of the printers' union in Scotland.*

   Attempts to establish a national printers' union in Scotland began in 1836. Eventually the Scottish Typographical Association (STA) was founded in 1853. It included small offices in towns where there was a moderate amount of printing activity. The STA had a continuous existence from 1853, but there were still inequalities between offices in terms of number of members, strength, and administration.

2. *Education reform in Zambia.*

   In the decade after independence, the high price of copper allowed the government to finance a large expansion of education and other social services. Zambia's first development plan set the ambitious goal of providing primary school facilities for all children by 1970. There was also an emphasis on getting urban and rural children through seven grades of primary school. This rapid expansion, combined with a large teacher training program, was a huge task.

2 **Analyze discourse:** Look back at Activity 1. Find some noun modifiers that are examples of the following types and write them down.

1. noun before the head noun: _printers',_
2. prepositional phrase after the head noun: _in Scotland,_
3. adjective phrase after the head noun: _____

3 **Practice writing:** The sentences are from an article about a political experiment. Combine each group of simple sentences to make a longer and more natural-sounding sentence. Use a variety of modifiers from Sections C and D. You may need to omit some words and phrases to make your new sentence grammatical. When you are finished, compare your sentences with a partner's. Answers may be different.

1. D.T. Campbell is a famous social scientist. He once designed a social experiment. It included several towns. The towns were divided into two groups. The groups were based on citizen characteristics.

   D. T. Campbell, a famous social scientist, once designed a social experiment with several towns
   divided into two groups based on citizen characteristics.

2. Each town had a newspaper. The newspapers were persuaded to participate in the experiment.

_____

3. They wrote phony articles. The articles were about political candidates. They contained information about their ideas and popularity. The information was false.

_____

_____

4. Scientists made comparisons. The comparisons covered the two groups of towns. Each town had citizens. The citizens answered questions about the candidates so the scientists could make the comparisons.

_____

_____

4 | **Practice writing:** What is your ideal situation? Be as descriptive as possible to describe exactly what you want. Circle the head nouns and underline each noun modifier as you write them.

1. I am looking for a roommate who is quiet, loves dogs, and is a college student.

2. _____

_____

3. _____

_____

Now with a partner think of three other topics. Write your own descriptions of what your ideal would be and compare it with your partner's ideal.

Voter registration procedures
Adjectives and Nouns to Modify a Noun

What have you learned from your grammar textbook?

When an **adjective** occurs before a noun, we say that it **modifies the noun**:

- *beautiful* flowers
- *blue* sky
- *happy* baby

A **noun** can also **modify another noun**, acting like an adjective:

- *grammar* book
- *vegetable* soup
- *car* shop

What does the corpus show?

A   In **informational writing** (newspaper and academic writing), many noun phrases include a modifier. Adjectives are extremely common. But surprisingly, **nouns as modifiers are almost as common as adjectives**.

B   **The most common adjectives** in writing express **many different functions**.

Function	Common Adjectives				Examples	
1. describing **size**	*big* *great*	*high* *large*	*little* *long*	*low* *small*	• *high* risk • *large* amounts	• *little* fear of reprisal • *small* businesses
2. describing **time** or **age**	*new* *old*	*young*			• a *new* law • the *old* town	• *young* children
3. expressing **evaluation**	*best* *good*	*important* *main*	*major* *right*	*special*	• a *good* education • the *main* concern	• the *right* direction • a *special* process
4. describing **relationship**	*different* *final*	*full* *general*	*same* *single*	*whole*	• a *different* story • *final* approval	• the *general* public • the *same* questions
5. identifying **topic** or **type**	*economic* *international*	*national* *political*	*public* *social*		• *economic* reform • *national* policy	• *political* influence • *social* benefits

C   **The most common nouns** used as **modifiers** in writing express **different kinds of functions** from adjectives. They often refer to **abstract entities** that you cannot actually see (e.g., *government, business, health, defense*). Such entities are commonly discussed in writing, making these noun-noun sequences especially important.

Function	Common Nouns Used as Modifiers				Examples	
1. identifying **institutions**	*church* *city* *community*	*court* *government* *hospital*	*office* *police* *prison*	*school* *state* *world*	• *community* groups • *government* agencies	• *police* officer • *world* trade
2. describing **home** or **family**	*baby* *car*	*child* *family*	*food* *home*	*tax* *water*	• *car* insurance • *food* prices	• *home* buyers • *water* bill

Function	Common Nouns Used as Modifiers				Examples	
3. describing **business**	*bank* *business* *company*	*computer* *consumer* *insurance*	*labor* *management* *market*	*price* *trade*	• **bank** policy • **company** profits	• **market** forces • **price** hikes
4. describing **conflict**	*army* *defense*	*emergency* *safety*	*security* *terrorist*	*war*	• **army** base • **safety** equipment	• **security** guard • **war** zone
5. identifying **the media**	*movie* *newspaper*	*press* *telephone*	*television* *TV*		• **newspaper** stories	• **TV** ads
6. describing **health**	*cancer*	*drug*	*health*		• **drug** addict	• **health** care
7. describing **time**	*day* *holiday*	*morning* *night*	*summer* *weekend*		• **day** care center	• **summer** heat
8. describing **sports**	*football* *soccer*	*sports*	*team*		• **soccer** match	• **sports** reporter

Activities

1 **Notice in context:** Read these two paragraphs from informational writing. Circle all nouns and adjectives that modify nouns. Underline the noun that is being modified.

1. **Newspaper writing:** *From an article describing the economy.*

   In December, energy prices plunged 1.4% after remaining steady the previous month. Further declines are probably ahead because of warm winter weather. Prices of gasoline and home heating oil both fell. Food prices also fell last month and during all of 1991.

2. **Academic writing:** *From a text about primary school education.*

   In each of the National Curriculum foundation subjects, there are primary school teachers with specialized knowledge. Out of 160,000 teachers, some 20,000 have qualifications in science, and 16,000 in math, with 40,000 in English. However, they and others with specialized skills are officially given only 40 minutes a week away from their home classes to develop specialized teaching programs related to their skill area.

2 **Analyze discourse:** Look back at Activity 1 and at the modifiers you circled. First, label each modifier as either an adjective (**A**) or a noun (**N**). Then list the modifiers that describe the following:

a. **Institutions:** _____

b. **Time:** _____

List two more functions and provide examples:

c. (*Other:* _____): _____

d. (*Other:* _____): _____

3 **Practice the structure:** Complete the paragraphs with modifiers from Sections B and C. When a blank is followed by (**N**), fill it with a noun; when a blank is followed by (**A**), fill it with an adjective.

1. *From a textbook about learning language.*

   You can practice listening both in and out of the classroom. Radio or _____ (**N**)
   programs offer good opportunities to listen to language. In the classroom, when you hear
   _____ (**A**) language, always listen several times before repeating. Participating in
   _____ (**N**) activities with local residents will also help improve comprehension.

2. *From an economic report about farming in Wales.*

   Tourism played a significant role in many farms with cottages, which were all being rented during the
   _____ (**N**) period. Other _____ (**N**) opportunities included growing
   grass for dairies and for sheep, which was the main source of income. However, dry seasons with very
   _____ (**A**) rainfall presented a serious risk.

4 **Practice writing:** Read the newspaper advice column about Carol's problem. Then write your advice. Use at least three adjectives and two nouns that modify nouns. You can use the adjectives and nouns suggested in the box or others that you think of. Circle each adjective or noun modifier, and underline the noun that is being modified.

> *Carol just got married, and she is worried about the strict financial rules in her new relationship. What should she do?*
>
> Carol must pay half of the household bills every month, and her medical insurance and income taxes are her own responsibility. When she and her new husband take vacations together, she must pay for her own expenses. And, oh yes, Carol is expected to buy all her own clothes and pay for any gifts she purchases for family members. Carol's friends are concerned about what she may be getting into with this new relationship. Carol asked for my opinion.

emergency	holiday	important	new	same	unfair
health	home	marriage	right	tax	water

EXAMPLE

Carol needs to ask herself some (important) questions about what she wants from the relationship . . .

_____

_____

_____

_____

_____

A question which is often asked
Adjective Clauses and Relative Pronoun Choice

What have you learned from your grammar textbook?

Adjective clauses (also called "relative clauses") are used to **modify a noun**. An adjective clause usually **begins with a relative pronoun** (*who, which, that*, etc.).

There are several options for **relative pronoun choice** in an adjective clause: **(1)** *who* is used for people; **(2)** *which* is used for things; and **(3)** *that* is used for both people and things.

    1. the **man** *who I saw*   **2.** the **cup** *which is on the table*   **3.** the **book** *that I read*

The **relative pronoun** can be the **subject (S)** or the **object (O)** of the verb in the adjective clause.

                 S V   O S V
- the guy *that looks* like Charlie   • the guy *that I saw* last week

When the **relative pronoun** is the **object** of the verb, it is **often omitted**.

- the guy *I saw* last week

What does the corpus show?

A   **Different relative pronouns** are preferred for **different uses** depending on the **meaning, grammatical context,** and **register** (conversation or writing).

B   **Relative pronouns** that refer to **a person** who is the **subject** of the verb in the adjective clause:

Pronoun	Description of Use	Examples
who	• common in conversation • the most common choice in writing	• The **people** *who were always doing everything* got tired. • A **doctor** *who lacks confidence* will put the patient at risk.
that	• common in conversation • rare in writing	• He's the **guy** *that always wears blue jeans.*

C   **Relative pronouns** that refer to **a person** who is the **object** of the verb in the adjective clause:

Pronoun	Description of Use	Examples
Ø*	• the most common choice in both conversation and writing	• You're the one **person** *I can talk to.* • Nosair met the **woman** *he married* at a Pittsburgh mosque.
that	• used occasionally in conversation • rare in writing	• Well this **man** *that she's engaged to* has been around for three years now.
whom	• very **rare** in conversation • rare in writing	• In economic and statistical terms, **people** *whom we define as old* are usually over 65.

*Ø = no relative pronoun

Be careful! Many textbooks say *who* is a common informal replacement for *whom*. It is occasionally used in conversation, but *that* is more common, and *no relative pronoun* is by far the most common choice.

D **Relative pronouns** that describe **a thing**:

Pronoun	Description of Use	Examples
which	• rare in conversation • the most common choice in **British English writing**	• The trust is a **charity** *which* helps those who *describe themselves as New Age Travellers.*
that	• common in conversation • the most common choice in **American English writing**	• They were all the **songs** *that* I thought you like. • The reprint contained two **cartoons** *that* had not *appeared with the original series.*
Ø*	• relatively common in conversation • rare in writing, but sometimes used when the **subject** of the adjective clause is a **personal pronoun**	• The last **thing** *we want to do* is irritate your elbow. • This task will be part of her work with the **company** *she* co-founded.

*Ø = no relative pronoun

Activities

1 **Notice in context:** Read the conversation and the paragraph from an academic text. Circle the relative pronouns and underline the adjective clauses.

1. **Conversation:** *About applying to a teacher's college.*

    CLERK: You need to go in there and fill out the application for teacher's education. Then they'll give you a packet that has all your financial information.

    STUDENT: Where do I find information about, um, class times?

    CLERK: Uh, the man who makes the schedule is out. Can you come by tomorrow?

2. **Academic writing:** *About the history of women in society.*

    Wealthy women also had special economic concerns that affected their marriage choices. Their social and economic status depended first on their fathers and later on their husbands. The economic status of even those educated women who worked was low in relation to that of educated men.

2 **Analyze discourse:** The following sentences were found in separate conversations, and they all contain adjective clauses with no relative pronouns. Underline the adjective clauses and write the most common choice for a relative pronoun that could begin the relative clause. If the most common choice is no pronoun, write **Ø**.

___Ø___ 1. I need to write her, but there are so many people I haven't written. I've just been so busy.

_____ 2. I found out today that the doctor doesn't accept patients after seven thirty. So I was the last one he saw.

_____ 3. Isn't that the most amazing thing you've ever seen? [*After a fireworks display.*]

_____ 4. Hospital staff try very hard to give patients food they like and can digest comfortably.

_____ 5. I saw that guy from Boston last night, the nicest guy I have ever met.

_____ 6. Our house isn't really in a good location anymore. It seems like every place I have to go is on the other side of town.

3 **Practice writing:** Complete this writing sample by an English learner. Write an appropriate relative pronoun (or write Ø for no pronoun) in each blank. Use each of the following options at least once: *that, which, who, Ø.*

Culture Shock

When I moved to America three years ago, I felt excited, scared, and happy. It took me a long time to get used to American food. Right now, the thing _____ I like best is chicken McNuggets. The other difference _____ I noticed is that in Taiwan people live in tall buildings _____ are built close together, but in LA people live in houses _____ have yards with flowers and trees. Now I'm living in San Marino. Although America is not my native country, I like living here, because of the contact with people _____ have different cultures. I have many friends here _____ I like a lot.

4 **Practice conversation:** Work with a partner. Describe a person or an object in the room so that your partner can guess who or what it is. Find at least three people or objects to describe and take turns with your partner describing and guessing. Use adjective clauses and the most common relative pronoun choices.

EXAMPLES

I see a **man who** is wearing brown socks and green shoes.
I see **something that** is round and has many colored shapes on it.
I see a **person I've known** for seven years.

That's the way I look at it
Adjective Clauses with Adverb Meanings

What have you learned from your grammar textbook?

Adjective clauses can be used to modify nouns that refer to time or place.

Adjective clauses about place usually begin with ***where, in which,*** or ***that.***

- That's the **house** *where* I live.
- That's the **house** *in which* I live.
- That's the **house** *that* I live in.

Adjective clauses about time can use ***when, that,*** or **no relative pronoun**.

- I remember the **day** *when* he left.
- I remember the **day** *that* he left.
- I remember the **day** he left.

What does the corpus show?

A **Adjective clauses** cover **four types** of adverb meaning: **place, time, reason,** or **manner** (how something is done). Although it is *possible* for these adjective clauses to modify many different nouns and to use many different relative pronouns, **each type** of clause has **particular common patterns**.

B Adjective clauses describing **places:**

Common Pattern	Description of Use	Examples
1. **noun of place** + *where* (physical place)	• common in conversation and writing • especially common with the noun *place*	• We should be getting to the **place** *where the highways diverge.* • They continued literacy training in the **communities** *where they lived.*
2. **noun** + *where* (not physical place, but logical meaning)	• common in academic writing • especially common with the noun *case*(s)	• There are a number of **cases** *where receptionists behave informally towards guests.*
3. **noun of place** + *that* OR **noun of place** + Ø*	• very common in conversation	• What's a cheaper **place** *that we could go?* • Where was that **restaurant** *we had dinner at?*
4. **noun of place** + *in / to which*	• typically used only in academic writing	• The bird makes a well-insulated **place** *in which to lay eggs.*

*Ø = no relative pronoun

C Adjective clauses describing **times:**

Common Pattern	Description of Use	Examples
1. **noun of time** + Ø	• common in conversation and writing	• My grandfather was bald by the **time** *he was thirty.* • That was the **day** *he left.*
2. **noun of time** + *when*	• less common	• Tell us about the **time** *when you got stuck on the road in Nevada.*

D Adjective clauses describing **reasons:**

Common Pattern	Description of Use	Examples
1. *reason* (n.) + *why*	• common in **conversation** and **writing**, especially: ***There is no reason why***	• This may be the **reason *why*** a theory *is lacking.* • **There's no reason *why*** you shouldn't *eat a chicken.*
2. *reason* (n.) + Ø	• common in **conversation**	• The only **reason** *we went there* was because we liked the people.

E Adjective clauses describing **manner of doing something:**

Common Pattern	Description of Use	Examples
1. *way* (n.) + Ø	• common in **conversation** and **writing**	• That's the **way** *I look at it.* • Aspects of context influence the **way** *law reports are formed.*
2. *way* (n.) + *that*	• common in **conversation** and **writing** (except academic writing)	• Here's a **way *that*** you could use it. • This is a change in the **way *that*** computers *are organized.*
3. *way* (n.) + *in which*	• generally common only in **academic writing**	• They provide a **way *in which*** they may be *more clearly understood.*

Activities

1 **Notice in context:** Read the conversation and the two paragraphs from different types of writing. Circle the nouns modified by adjective clauses with adverb meanings. Underline the adjective clauses.

1. **Conversation:** *After a meeting.*

   ALEJO: Hey, can I get a ride?

   SALWA: Yeah, but you have to promise not to comment on the cleanliness of my car or the way I drive.

2. **Fiction writing:** *Disappointment after the wedding.*

   Their honeymoon in Acapulco was a disaster. The surroundings were beautiful, but Eddie drank all day and gambled all night. Back in London things worsened, and by the time they moved into Lady Elizabetta's flat Rafaella had grown to hate her husband, and yet she had no idea how she could escape.

3. **Academic writing:** *Advice to language learners regarding listening/speaking practice.*

   Listening can be done in a classroom-type situation where you listen to a live language helper or to a recording which can be played over and over again. Or it can be done outside the classroom—in any place where people are talking and you can listen. It is good to seek out opportunities where you can listen without being called upon to participate, for example, radio or TV programs, sermons, public speeches, in the village circle at night, and participating in community activities. In the classroom, when you obtain new data from a language helper, always listen several times before mimicking.

2 **Analyze discourse:** Look back at Activity 1. Decide whether each adjective clause indicates physical place, logical meaning, time, reason, or manner. Write *P* (place), *L* (logical meaning), *T* (time), *R* (reason), or *M* (manner), next to the clause.

3 **Practice the structure:** Complete the sentences with the appropriate words or phrases from the box. Use nouns and adjective clauses that are common for the type of writing or conversation. There may be more than one answer.

in which	time	way	where	Ø (no pronoun)
to which	time when	way that	reason why	

1. Pauli envied the _____ his elder brother could make friends so easily. (FICT.)

2. If the historical section of your thesis ends up being much too long, there is no _____ it cannot be edited and rewritten. (ACAD.)

3. Households were selected for the survey in a _____ gave all phone numbers, listed and unlisted, an equal chance of being included. (NEWS)

4. Clearly this is an area _____ considerable further work is required. (ACAD.)

5. STUDENT: Are bus passes here?

   CLERK: No, we don't sell any bus passes here.

   STUDENT: Oh . . . there's nowhere near to buy one, I suppose?

   CLERK: The closest place _____ I know of is the University, but I think they're closed until Tuesday.

4 **Practice conversation:** Work with a partner. Ask and answer these questions. In each answer, include a noun modified by an adjective clause which has the meaning given in parentheses.

1. Where was your first job, or where do you hope it will be? (**physical place**)
2. I get done working at 9 tonight. What will you be doing then? (**time**)
3. How do you like to cook chicken? (**manner**)

5 **Practice writing:** Write your answers to these questions, using complete sentences. In each answer, include a noun modified by an adjective clause which has the meaning given in parentheses. Share your answers with a partner.

1. Should English instructors always give tests? (**logical meaning** of *where*; in your answer, describe a case where an instructor might not give a test)

   _____

   _____

   _____

   _____

2. Should your instructors give you homework every night? (**reasons**)

   _____

   _____

   _____

Is there anything I can do?
Pronouns Modified by Adjective Clauses

What have you learned from your grammar textbook?

Adjective clauses (also called "relative clauses") are used to (**1**) **modify** a **noun**. They can also be used after (**2**) an **indefinite pronoun** or (**3**) the demonstrative pronoun *those*. The adjective clause usually begins with a relative pronoun, although it can sometimes be omitted.

1. The **book** *that I read* was very exciting.   OR   The **book** *I read* was very exciting.
2. He saw **someone** *who looked suspicious*.
3. **Those** *who failed the test* should speak to the teacher.

What does the corpus show?

A It is very **common** for **certain pronouns** to be **modified by adjective clauses**. The patterns **vary** in conversation and informational writing (newspaper and academic writing).

B The indefinite pronoun *one* modified by an adjective clause:

	Description of Use	Examples
1. conversation	• common • often used with relative pronoun **that** or **no relative pronoun** • used to specify "which one"	• The **one** *that he gave me* is like a Swiss army knife. • Is this the **one** *he had?*
2. informational writing	• very common • **that, who**, and **which** are the most common relative pronouns • used to add information about a noun that was already named	• The most stable free radical is the **one** *that predominates.* • The most satisfactory system is **one** *which indicates the structure of the compound.* • They are the **ones** *that must change.*

C Other indefinite pronouns (i.e., *someone, somebody, something, etc.*) modified by adjective clauses:

	Description of Use	Examples
1. conversation	• somewhat common • often used with relative pronoun **that** or **no relative pronoun** • adjective clauses are usually short • *anything I can do* is often used in offers of help	• I bet he's waiting for **something** *that he wants.* • **Nobody** *I know* is ever gonna hear this. • And there was **nothing** *you could do about it.* • Call if there is **anything** *I can do.*
2. informational writing	• very common • a great variety in relative pronouns (see Unit 41), but **that** is most common	• People think that heart attacks are **something** *that you die from.* • The supplier can provide solutions to **anyone** *who uses open systems.*

Be careful! In conversation, "sentence relatives" are common after an indefinite pronoun. These clauses **modify the entire sentence**, not just the indefinite pronoun (*see Unit 47*).

• We try to control **everything**, *which is pretty tough to do.*

D The demonstrative pronoun *those* modified by an adjective clause:

	Description of Use	Examples
1. conversation	• uncommon • occasionally used in proverbs or jokes	• There are three kinds of people: **those** *who make things happen*, **those** *who* watch *things happen*, and **those** *who wonder what happened*.
2. informational writing	• very common • **who** and **which** are the most common relative pronouns • the adjective clause identifies a person or object	• The state of Wyoming doesn't sell coal but taxes **those** *who extract it*. • The schools that are highly regarded are **those** *which have found ways of involving teachers in decisions*.

Activities

1 **Notice in context:** Read the conversation and the paragraph from an academic text. Circle indefinite or demonstrative pronouns and underline any adjective clauses that modify them.

1. **Conversation:** *About the music at a party.*

   NICOLE: Do you have something that's a little more upbeat?

   KATHI: There's a bunch of CD's over there.

   NICOLE: Uh, do you want to listen to anything?

   KATHI: Yeah. There's that really good one that we heard a few days ago.

2. **Academic writing:** *About attitudes in the classroom.*

   As the teacher gets to know the class she should become aware of the individual personalities of the students. She should pay attention to those who are afraid in certain situations; the ones with few ideas who need help and to be given extra confidence and encouragement; the timid ones who need to be urged to take a leading role; and the students who respond well to a challenge. The teacher needs to observe whether or not these students are interacting in constructive ways that lead to learning.

2 **Analyze discourse:** Read the sentences and underline the adjective clauses that modify indefinite or demonstrative pronouns. Then explain the relative pronoun choice for each clause. Is the relative pronoun typical for the register (conversation or academic writing) and indefinite pronoun that it refers to? Write your explanation on the line.

1. He said criticism "is something that is uncomfortable, but it is something that I'll have to live with." (NEWS)

   _____

2. I wonder if there's somebody I could call. (CONV.)

   _____

3. Teachers regard the activity as educational—one which supplements classroom education by exposing the students to diverse views. (NEWS)

   _____

4. There was nothing that we wanted to watch on TV. (CONV.)

_____

5. They were faced with the impossible task of finding something that was cheap. (ACAD.)

_____

6. Is this the one you're looking for? (CONV.)

_____

3 **Practice the structure:** Complete the paragraph from a newspaper article about a burglary. Fill out each blank with an adjective clause that modifies the boldfaced pronoun. Use the words in parentheses. When you are finished compare your story with a partner's.

After Police Responded to a Complaint about a Noisy Couple

When the police returned to the station after talking to the couple, an officer remarked that the refrigerator in the neighbors' kitchen resembled **one**

_that had been taken during a burglary at a nearby house_____.

1. *(taken / burglary/ house/ nearby)*

Following their suspicions, the officers discovered **something**

_____

2. *(confirmed / theories / neighborhood / about)*

After an investigation revealed that one of the neighbors was wanted for several crimes, including burglary, the officers returned to search the house to look for **anything**

_____

3. *(connected / neighbor / crimes / other)*

They found many promising clues, but the **one**

_____

4. *(police / found / shocking / most)*

led the officers' investigation in a completely new direction. A surprising twist to the story was about to unfold, and it was **nothing**

_____

5. *(any / ever / officers / foreseen)*

4 **Practice writing:** Write descriptions of the objects and people listed. Use indefinite pronouns and ***those*** followed by adjective clauses. When you are finished, think of other objects or people to describe. Then with a partner, take turns guessing what is described.

1. jacket: _It's something that keeps you warm. I have one that has four pockets._
There are those that have hoods and those that do not.

2. telephone: _____

3. TV reporter: _____

4. teapot: _____

5. travel agent: _____

6. *(other)* _____

7. *(other)* _____

8. *(other)* _____

9. *(other)* _____

10. *(other)* _____

I've got a lot to do
Noun + Infinitive

What have you learned from your grammar textbook?

Nouns (N) can be followed by an **adjective phrase (AP)** functioning as a noun modifier:

      N   AP
- The *girls* **sitting on the bench** are my sisters.
- The *book* **used in this class** is interesting.
- It is *time* **to stop working.**

What does the corpus show?

A   **Infinitives** can be used **in adjective phrases that modify nouns**. They are **slightly more common in conversation** than in writing. Other kinds of adjective phrases and adjective clauses are much more common in writing (*see Unit 39 for an overview of noun modifiers in writing*).

- The best *thing* **to do** is call.
- He hasn't had *time* **to talk**.

B   In conversation, **only a few nouns** are commonly modified by infinitives. These nouns are very **general in meaning** (*see Units 19 and 20 for more on general nouns in conversation*). In a noun + infinitive combination, the **infinitive expresses specific information** and makes the message clearer than the noun alone would.

Meaning Category	Noun (+ Infinitive)	Example
1. objects	*thing* *stuff* *a lot*	• It wasn't a real sensitive *thing* **to say**. • I was making *stuff* **to drink**. • I've got *a lot* **to do**.
2. time	*time*	• This is a good *time* **to have a break** before we finish for today. • It's *time* **to eat**.
3. place	*place* *places*	• What a horrible *place* **to work**! • I've got *places* **to go**.
4. **manner** of doing something	*way**	• Find a better *way* **to say this**.

*Way can also mean "distance," usually in *a long way to go*: We've got *a long way to go*.

C   Most infinitive phrases do not have a subject stated in them because the subject is clear from the context. However, **occasionally the subject of the infinitive is stated** in a prepositional phrase with *for*:

Reason for Subject	Phrase with Subject	Phrase without Subject
1. emphasizes the **speaker or listener**, rather than making a more general statement	• That's a hard thing *for me* **to do**. [I do a hard thing.]	• That's a hard thing **to do**. [Implies it is hard for anyone.]
2. states a subject that is **not the speaker or listener**	• It's time *for the leaves* **to fall off** the trees, isn't it? [The leaves fall off the trees.]	• It's time **to fall off** the trees. [Means that the speaker and listener will fall off the trees!]

D In **academic writing**, **most nouns** modified by infinitive phrases are **more specific** than the general nouns in conversation. For example, the nouns *evidence* and *assumption* are abstract, but they are more specific than *thing* or *stuff*:

- There is *evidence* **to suggest** that we should control for age when assessing the impact of income.
- This is too general an *assumption* **to make**.

However, the general nouns *time* and *way* are also common with infinitives in writing:

- Sedimentation must have been fast enough to bury the tree before the tree had *time* **to rot**.
- One obvious *way* **to minimize** this problem is to reduce the number of different data formats.

Activities

1 **Notice in context:** Read the two excerpts from different conversations and the paragraph from an academic text. Underline the **noun + infinitive** combinations.

1. **Conversation:** *A dog trainer explains the advantages of a small cage (a "crate").*

   You can put your dog in its crate at nighttime, and you don't have to worry about it, and your dog has its own little special place to sleep and a quiet time to relax. I mean like a portable cage inside your house, to put your animal in. That's also the best way to housebreak your dog, is get a crate.

2. **Conversation:** *A field researcher misses a good opportunity.*

   When she first went to Dulce she was trying to find a place to stay there, and they made her this incredible offer. They said, you can stay in our portable housing for teachers, but you have to be a teacher's aide. She should have jumped on it because it would be a way for her to make friends and meet people, which you have to do before you can find an assistant and start getting data, but she wasn't thinking that way. She told them that she didn't have time to be a teacher's aide and then they all got insulted and everybody ignored her, the whole community.

3. **Academic writing:** *About a new medical discovery*

   We have seen evidence to suggest that this could be the first step in what will probably be a revolution in medicine over the next decade. Gene therapy, a new medical tool in the war on cancer and many inherited disorders, could be used on patients for the first time this fall. A scientist for the National Institute of Health said that if the technique works, it gives doctors a powerful new way to cure the incurable.

2 **Practice the structure:** Complete each one of these sentences from conversation or academic writing with a noun and an infinitive from the appropriate box. Use each infinitive only once.

1. **Conversation.**

   > NOUNS: *time   thing   place   stuff*   INFINITIVES: *to eat   to do   to ask   to go   to study*

   a. The best ____time to study____ for any test is early in the morning.
   b. If you're gonna take a tropical vacation, the _____ is Hawaii.
   c. Cake doesn't sound like a particularly healthful _____ for breakfast.
   d. The boss just put these files on my desk. I've got plenty of _____ before I leave tonight.
   e. Now is the _____ what could happen if you go ahead with this plan.

2. Academic writing.

NOUNS: *time*   *way*   *assumption*   INFINITIVES: *to make*   *to read*   *to introduce*

a. Studying Latin grammar and vocabulary is an easy _____ general linguistic concepts to language learners.

b. In the world of traditional physics, it was the natural _____ that energy flowed in and out of space in a perfectly continuous way.

c. A series of passages were read by adults in a reading comprehension study, with the _____ each sentence being measured.

3 **Practice conversation:** Work with a partner. Take turns asking each question and responding with a **noun + infinitive** combination that makes sense. A meaning category is suggested in parentheses for each one. Write your answers after you say them.

1. A: When do you think we should take our trip to New England? **(time)**
B: _The best **time to go** is in the fall, when the leaves are changing color._ _____

2. A: I'm going to do laundry. Do you have dirty clothes? **(object)**
B: _____

3. A: Should I buy a big screen TV now, or wait until they're cheaper? **(time)**
B: _____

4. A: What college do you recommend for math? **(place)**
B: _____

5. A: What can I do to get my kids to eat their vegetables? **(manner of doing something)**
B: _____

The approach used in nursing
Adjective Phrases

Academic Writing

What have you learned from your grammar textbook?

When an **adjective clause** has a **subject relative pronoun**, the clause can often be changed to an **adjective phrase**: (1) an *–ing* phrase, (2) an *-ed* phrase, or (3) an **appositive** noun phrase.

Adjective Clause		Adjective Phrase
1. the girl *who is running* around the track	→	the girl *running* around the track
2. the agreement *which was discussed* at the meeting	→	the agreement *discussed* at the meeting
3. Nawaz Sharif, *who is* Prime Minister of Pakistan	→	Nawaz Sharif, *Prime Minister of Pakistan*

What does the corpus show?

A **Adjective phrases** are as **common** as adjective clauses in academic writing. They are rare in conversation.

B **Adjective clauses** almost **never include a present progressive verb**. Instead writers use an *-ing* **adjective phrase.**

• Bank regulators soon will ease standards *governing* real estate appraisals.
NOT: ~~Bank regulators soon will ease standards *which are governing* real estate appraisals.~~

C **Frequency information.** Most of the **verbs that are common in** *-ing* **adjective phrases** rarely occur as main clause progressive verbs. These are **non-action** (stative) verbs.

Verbs (* = very common)		Examples
arising	*involving**	• Procedures *concerning* office machinery are carried out efficiently.
*concerning** *relating*		• Households *containing* an elderly member are exempt.
consisting *requiring*		• Gift-giving constitutes an exchange *having* special characteristics.
*containing** *resulting*		• An alternative system *involving* nurses has also been evaluated.
*having** *using**		• Reports *using* the WADA technique have provided little counterevidence.
*including**		

Be careful! It is possible to use these **same verbs in the simple present, in a full adjective clause.** However, *-ing* adjective phrases are much more common for these verbs. When a full relative clause does occur, it is often a **non-restrictive** (non-essential) **clause**:

• The cost of installing open systems technology, *which contains* more options, is likely to be more than the cost of installing established proprietary solutions.

D **Frequency information.** The **verbs that are common in** *-ed* **adjective phrases** are also common as main clause **passives**.

Verbs (* = very common)		Examples
*based**	*obtained*	• Approximation techniques *based* on "heuristic" rules are frequently
caused	*produced*	employed in these situations.
concerned	*taken*	[PASSIVE: the . . . techniques *are based* on . . .]
*given**	*used**	• This system complements the approach *used* in nursing care planning.
made		[PASSIVE: the approach *is used* in . . .]

E Appositive noun phrases are **common in** academic writing but rare in conversation. They often occur in parentheses.

Function	Example
1. explaining a **technical term**	• It can lead to **hypocalcaemia** *(a deficiency of calcium in the blood)*.
2. introducing an **abbreviation**	• The ratios in the **caesium chloride** *(CsCl)* crystal lattices are 1:1.
3. providing **information about a proper noun**	• The information is being put together by the **Central Computer Agency,** *a body which advises government departments on equipment purchases.*
4. providing a **list of items** in a group	• Univariate analysis was undertaken to examine the effect of a number of individual patient **characteristics** *(age, sex, body mass index, smoking)*.

Activities

1 **Notice in context:** Read the two paragraphs from different academic texts. First, underline each adjective phrase and draw an arrow to the noun it modifies. Be careful! Adverbs may occur between the adjective phrases and the nouns they modify. Second, circle the verbs in the adjective phrases that are related to passive voice verbs.

1. *From an instructional manual about building materials.*

   Both the stands and supports of display boards commonly used for advertisements in the cities are mostly constructed of wood . . . Wood, the most suitable and most popular material for furniture, is comparatively cheaper than metal.

2. *From an article about methods of communication.*

   One problem arising from the use of electronic communication results from the fact that procedures previously settled with paper letters and telephone calls are now also carried out through new electronic methods. This implies that correspondence concerning the same task may be contained in three different types of media (telephone, paper, and electronic media) and may become disjointed.

2 **Analyze discourse:** Read these sentences from academic writing. Underline each appositive noun phrase. Then label its function: Write **T** (explaining a technical term), **A** (introducing an abbreviation), **I** (providing information about a proper noun), or **L** (providing a list of items in a class) next to the phrase.

1. Linguist I.A. Richards distinguishes four types of functions of language and four kinds of meaning (sense, feeling, tone, and intention).

2. Magnetic resonance imaging (MRI) has evolved over the past decade as an important new technique, providing additional information to that obtained with standard medical investigations.

3. It is still an adventure to travel down the canyon of the Colorado River in a small boat, repeating the first trip made in 1869 by Major John W. Powell, a geologist who later helped found the U.S. Geological Survey (USGS).

4. The cotton crop is attacked by black-arm which is caused by a bacteria which also causes angular leaf spot, a disease that affects all above-ground parts of the plant.

3 **Practice the structure:** Complete each sentence with the correct form of one of the verbs from the box.

base	give	require	obtain	use	contain	include	concern

1. In a vocabulary game, the computer might produce a list of words _____ one the child hasn't learned, and the child must locate that word. All other words in the list should be familiar to the child.

2. During photosynthesis, water is oxidized by the removal of hydrogen, and oxygen is released (a process _____ energy to break the chemical bonds between the hydrogen and oxygen).

3. One might say that the "candid camera" technique _____ in some television programs, where people have tricks played on them for the benefit of the viewers, is a source of observation for social scientists.

4. Because of difficult technical terminology, all medical information _____ to patients by doctors may not be fully understood and may require additional explanation.

5. Another drink from the coconut is the juice or wine _____ by tapping the unopened flowers.

4 **Practice writing:** For each of the following topics, choose a subject that interests you and write a short informative paragraph about it on a separate piece of paper. Use each of these types of adjective phrases at least once: *-ed, -ing* and appositive noun phrases. Include at least two adjective phrases in each description. Underline the adjective phrases.

1. Music
2. Recreation
3. Diet
4. Literature (e.g., books, magazines, newspapers, etc.)

EXAMPLES
Music <u>produced with fiddles and banjos</u> is often called Bluegrass . . .
Tetherball <u>(a leather ball attached to a tall metal pole with a long cord)</u> is a popular schoolyard game . . .
Diets <u>consisting of very few calories</u> are rarely effective . . .
Books <u>written during a period of depression or frustration in an author's life</u> can be funny and uplifting.

A number of reasons
Prepositional Phrases Modifying Nouns

Informational Writing

What have you learned from your grammar textbook?

Prepositions show "physical" relationships such as **location** or **direction**. They are often combined with a noun or noun phrase to make **prepositional phrases.**

- I saw the lamp *on the table*.
- I put the book *in the box*.
- I gave the pen *to my friend*.

What does the corpus show?

A In **informational writing**, **prepositional phrases** are by far the **most common type of noun modifier** occurring after the head noun (*see Unit 39*).

B **Frequency information.** Only **a few specific prepositions are especially common** in prepositional phrases that are **noun modifiers.**

Preposition	Frequency	Examples	
1. *of*	very frequent	• a set *of* books	• the style *of* interpretation
2. *in*	frequent	• variation *in* the sample	• a decrease *in* performance
3. *for*	frequent	• a school *for* disabled children	• a cure *for* AIDS
4. *on*	frequent	• restrictions *on* travel	• a book *on* pets

C Usually these **prepositions do not have their literal "physical" meaning**:

- These findings help to set a limit *on such generalizations*.
- This dependence has produced a change *in basic work practices*.

D In **informational writing**, we often find **complex structures**, with **several prepositional phrases** occurring in a **series**:

- a sudden increase *in demand for his product*
- the centre *of a cube with spheres at each corner*
- a preface *to a book on Kant by his friend and colleague Hamelin*

E Many common nouns tend to occur in combination with a specific preposition. You might want to learn these **noun + preposition combinations** as if they were a single word.

Pattern	Noun + Preposition Combinations			Examples
1. **noun + *of***	*amount of* *case of* *nature of*	*number of* *part of* *result of*	*type(s) of* *use of*	• a **number of** reasons for . . . • the **use of** computers
2. **noun + *in***	*change(s) in* *difference in*	*increase in* *interest in*	*reduction in* *variation in*	• an **increase in** fuel economy • **interest in** research
3. **noun + *for***	*basis for* *evidence for* *explanation for*	*need for* *potential for* *reason for*	*responsibility for* *support for*	• the **basis for** the agreement • the **need for** field surveys
4. **noun + *on***	*data on* *effect on*	*emphasis on* *studies on*	*information on* *influence on*	• no **effect on** the success rate • **emphasis on** global markets

F Many **nouns** actually occur as **fixed expressions with two specific prepositions** – one before and one after:

Pattern	Nouns Used in Pattern			Examples
1. *in the* _____ *of*	*absence* *area* *case*	*context* *form* *presence*	*process* *study*	• *in the absence of* a rationale • *in the case of* electronic media
2. *in* _____ *of*	*a number*	*terms*	*a variety*	• *in terms of* rational principles
3. *in* _____ *to*	*addition*	*contrast*	*relation*	• *in contrast to* other species
4. *as* _____ *of*	*a consequence*	*part*	*a result*	• *as a result of* these changes
5. *at the* _____ *of*	*beginning* *end*	*start*	*time*	• *at the end of* Chapter 6

Activities

1 Notice in context: Read the two paragraphs from different academic texts. Underline the prepositional phrases that modify nouns. Draw an arrow from the preposition to the noun that it modifies. Be careful! Some prepositions modify verbs.

1. *From the preface of a biology textbook.*

   Brief notes in the margins serve as slight amplifications of the text and as comments on the extraordinary personalities who have been a part of the quest to understand the Earth. We have increased the number of boxes of notes that expand some materials of the text. These boxes are for the student who wants to understand more deeply some of the background of the subject.

2. *From a book chapter about an insect population.*

   There is a need for more studies in typical parts of the Bombay Locust area for comparison with other areas; it is not possible otherwise to discover the reasons for a decrease in the population density of the locust that has occurred since 1908.

2 Analyze and edit: Read the following sentences written by English language learners and decide if each boldfaced **noun + preposition(s)** combination is correct. If the combination is correct, write *C* on the line; if it is incorrect, cross it out and write the correct combination on the line.

<u>in the form of</u> 1. His philosophy was that his cars had to have reliability **for the form of** simplicity and strength, rather than performance.

_____ 2. If airlines made a substantial **reduction on** fares there would be times when travelers would be unable to find seats on the flight of their choice.

_____ 3. Interviews were conducted and questionnaires were used to acquire **information on** the types of media used in advertising.

_____ 4. In this essay, I attempt to analyze the potential problems and the **need for** road-building in eastern Malaysia.

_____ 5. In recent times, there has been a renewed **interest for** the old traditions and the language of Scotland.

_____ 6. The **reasons of** my choice to move to New Zealand are these: I don't like too much sun, but I like winter and downhill skiing.

3 **Practice writing:** Use your own ideas to offer explanations for the information in the graph, which shows human population growth over the last 12,000 years. Write at least one sentence with a **noun + preposition(s)** combination for each of the meanings listed below. You can use one of the nouns in parentheses.

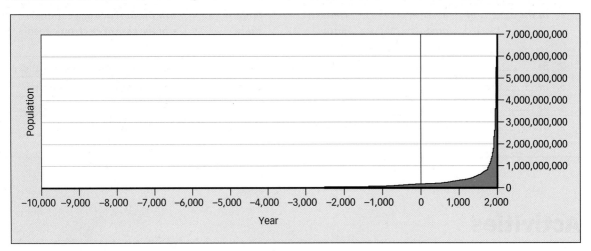

1. **Cause-effect** (possible nouns: *effect, reason, influence, result,* etc.):

   Medical developments in the last two hundred years have had a major **effect on** human population growth.

   _____

2. **Information** (possible nouns: *information, studies, study, data, interest* etc.):

   Information on the best farming practices has increased food supply and population in many countries.

   _____

3. **Change** (possible nouns: *change, reduction, increase, decrease,* etc.):

   _____

   _____

4. **Time** (possible nouns: *end, beginning, start,* etc.):

   _____

   _____

5. **Range** (possible nouns: *number, variety, amount, type,* etc.):

   _____

   _____

He saluted me, which I enjoyed
Adjective Clauses That Modify Sentences

What have you learned from your grammar textbook?

Adjective clauses usually modify the noun that they immediately follow. The relative pronoun **which** is used to **refer to things** (not people). **Adjective clauses that add descriptive information about a noun** but are **not essential** are punctuated with **commas**.

- Boston, **which is in the state of Massachusetts,** is an interesting city to visit.

What does the corpus show?

A Some adjective clauses do not modify a noun. Instead they **comment on the whole idea in the preceding clause**. They are called **"sentence relatives."** They always use **which**. When spoken, they have **intonation** that sets off the adjective clause. When written, **commas** are used to set off the adjective clause:

- Well, I don't have time to do it for this project, **which means it'll probably have to get put off until next year.**

Sentence relatives are **common** in **conversation**. They are also **common** in **newspaper** and **fiction writing**, but they are rare in academic writing.

B **Four functions** are expressed by sentence relatives. Two of these are very common.

Function (* = very common)	Example
1. expressing a **feeling** or **value judgment***	• On Mondays after the meeting, I count the money, **which I enjoy**. • She wants to be home for the kids, **which is great**.
2. commenting on **likelihood***	• Um I'm guessing there might be time to do it, though I'd have to leave work just a little bit early, **which is possible**.
3. explaining a **reason**	**A:** It was a good thing I went back cause I just found my wallet on the floor. **B:** Oh yeah. **A:** By the dresser, **which is probably why I didn't see it in the first place**.
4. interpreting **information**	• Federal Aviation Administration spokesperson Dick Stafford said the agency is in the final rule-making procedure, **which means it still could impose the rule as proposed, modify it, or withdraw it.**

C The **use of sentence relatives differs** between conversation and different types of writing.

	Description of Use	Examples
1. conversation	• sentence relatives are **more common** in conversation than other registers • usually used for feelings, value judgments, or likelihood	• She wants me to drive up and then drive back in a day, **which kind of irritates me.** • I had to redo my calculations, **which is good because I found about four that I did wrong**.

(continued on next page)

	Description of Use	Examples
2. newspaper and fiction writing	• **relatively common** • in newspapers, sentence relatives occur most often in **reviews and quotations** • sentence relatives occasionally **interpret information**	• "The market is bouncing back, ***which is probably the best news to happen in a long while***," one stock manager said. • Mostly, he spends his time trying to prove his extinction theory, ***which means long hours combing the dirt for bones***.
3. academic writing	• sentence relatives **rarely used** • **adjective + *to*-clause** or ***that*-clause** more common for value judgments and likelihood (*see Unit 36*)	

Activities

1 Notice in context: Read the two conversations and the paragraph from a newspaper article. Circle each sentence relative clause, and underline the independent clause that it modifies.

1. **Conversation:** *About an argument with a friend.*

   SULIM: Anyway, he called me back later and apologized, which is a real plus* for him.

   FAWAD: Yeah, that's amazing.

2. **Conversation:** *While in the car on a trip.*

   CARLA: I want to know where we are. Actually, I do believe that we can switch to the west Texas map now.

   SUZE: We are right around Colorado City, which is near Odessa where my best friend lives.

3. **Newspaper writing:** *Information about a popular basketball star.*

   Michael Jordan has some things going for him besides his nice-guy image. He has a college degree, which is more than can be said for some of our presidents. He was born in New York, raised in North Carolina, and lives in Chicago, which means he'd have national appeal. His basketball-playing style has been widely praised for its spontaneity.

   *****a real plus** is an idiom meaning "something good or positive"

2 Analyze discourse: Match each sentence relative in the passages on the left with the correct function on the right. Write the letter of the function on the line.

_____ **1.** It takes the body four hours to digest fats, which is why people often feel sluggish after eating.

_____ **2.** Kathryn didn't hear the alarm go off the next morning, which in itself was unusual. On days when she was due in the office early she normally was awake and out of bed long before her clock radio clicked itself on.

_____ **3.** I want to tell you about aerobics directors. Many of them are not full time, which means that they are usually running about from job to job to job just trying to make ends meet.

a. commenting on likelihood

b. interpreting information

c. expressing a feeling

d. making a value judgment

e. explaining a reason

3 **Practice conversation:** Work with a partner. Respond to each conversation opener. In each response, include a sentence relative with the function shown in parentheses. When you are finished, practice each conversation with your partner.

EXAMPLE

A: I haven't seen you since your surgery! How are you feeling?

B: Much better. I've gained a lot of weight, _which is good because I lost so much before_ .
(making a value judgment)

1. **A:** What do you think about Hawaii as a place to take a vacation?

   B: Well, there are lots of water sports to do there, _____ .
   (expressing a feeling)

2. **A:** Do you think we'll get over the mountains before it's snowing too hard?

   B: I think we'll be ok if we can keep going at this speed, _____ .
   (commenting on likelihood)

3. **A:** I know you like the new teacher, but I'm not convinced he's so great.

   B: He explains the answers to the homework, _____ .
   (making a value judgment)

4. **A:** I hear you got a job as a "Hospitality Coordinator." What is that, anyway?

   B: I have to meet and greet all our international guests, _____ .
   (interpreting information)

4 **Practice conversation:** Work with a partner. Read the lines of conversation about a trip to the beach. Notice the sentence relatives. Then respond to each line. Make sure your response shows an understanding of the function of the sentence relative. When you are finished, practice each conversation with your partner.

EXAMPLE

A: We should pack now, in case Pete wants to leave when he gets home, which is possible.

B: _Yeah, he'll probably want to leave right away._

1. **A:** I've gained a lot of weight, which is why my bathing suit doesn't fit any more.

   B: _____

2. **A:** Pete may not get home from work until 7:00 PM, which means we might not leave until 8:00.

   B: _____

3. **A:** I hope we don't have to drive after dark, which I really do not like.

   B: _____

Well, I better get going
Discourse Markers

What have you learned from your grammar textbook?

Spoken language sometimes has **different features than writing**. For example, **tag questions** are often used in conversation but not in writing.

- You eat ice cream every day, *don't you?*

What does the corpus show?

A One common feature of conversation is "**discourse markers**." Discourse markers are **short words or expressions** with **special organizing functions** in conversation. Each discourse marker has specific functions. This unit covers three of the common discourse markers in American English: *well, okay,* and *like.*

B The discourse marker *well* has **different functions** depending on its **position** (beginning or middle) **in a turn**:

Function	Example
BEGINNING OF A TURN: 1. indicating that a **contrast** is coming	A: I would love to live in Boulder. B: *Well I've been there, but it's also expensive, isn't it?*
2. indicating a **lack of certainty** or a **disagreement** (especially in answers)	A: Do you have to get new tires? B: *Well, probably. I haven't . . . I always forget to put air into them.*
3. indicating a **transition to ending** the conversation	A: I always liked that tie. It's Italian isn't it? B: Yeah. Good tie. A: *Well, I better get going.*
MIDDLE OF A TURN: 4. used during **self-correction** or when **thinking about ideas**	• I think I'll come back on um . . . *well,* we are leaving on the twelfth and I think that's a Tuesday morning, so I'll come back like the tenth.
5. used to **begin direct speech***	• I asked Kathy if she was still running and stuff and she says *well I guess you'd call it walking.*

* See Unit 37.

C The discourse marker *okay* has the following **four functions**:

Function	Example
1. indicating the **start of a new topic** or **sub-topic**, often in a long explanation	• There are five different categories. I'll just name the five and then we'll talk about each one a little bit separately. *Okay,* there's enumeration, advance labeling, reporting, recapitulation, and questions. *Okay,* and then going back to enumeration . . .
2. indicating a **transition to ending** a topic or conversation	A: *Okay,* you got the general idea? B: Got the general idea. A: *Okay,* see you Wednesday.

Function	Example
3. indicating **acknowledgement** of what the other person said	A: Divide the bill? [at a restaurant] B: Yeah. A: *Okay*.
4. used to **begin direct speech***	• I said *okay* Gus I can stay.

* See Unit 37.

D The discourse marker ***like*** has the following **two functions**:

Function	Example
1. indicating the next words are **not exact**	• I called them ***like*** *a hundred times.* • Luckily I found it the next day but I was ***like*** *panicked.*
2. indicating the next words are **especially important**	A: It was ***like*** *found a couple of days ago in someone's freezer.* B: I don't get it so . . . A: Because it was ***like*** *stolen.*

E **Be careful!** Words that function as discourse markers **also have other, different functions**. For example, ***well*** also often occurs as an **adverb** (*I did well*) or **adjective** (*I feel well*).

Activities

1 **Notice in context:** Read the two conversations. Circle ***well, okay,*** and ***like*** when they are used as discourse markers.

1. *The last ones to lock up and leave the office.*

   ZAYTA: I'm just like, nervous. I always like to make sure, take a second look, nothing under there, nothing strange.

   CHEONG: No, everything looks fine to me.

   ZAYTA: All right, well, listen, thank you so much for staying late.

   CHEONG: Well, then, I'll see you tomorrow.

   ZAYTA: Drive safely.

   CHEONG: Okay, thanks.

2. *An expensive wedding present.*

   ANDREA: That antique Chinese chest was like two hundred thousand dollars and he gave it to his wife as a wedding present, you know. It was like a lot of money.

   DAVID: Well, any time she wants to sell it, she can sell it for a lot, right?

   ANDREA: Or if it goes well with her furniture, keep it for a hundred or a couple hundred years. Besides, it's nice.

2 **Analyze discourse:** Look back at Activity 1 and at each discourse marker that you circled. Write its function (for example, ***lack of certainty*** or ***begins direct speech***) in the margin. Draw an arrow between the marker and its function. Some discourse markers may have more than one function. Discuss with a partner.

3 **Practice the structure:** Work with a partner. Complete the three conversations with appropriate discourse markers. Pay attention to each one's function. When there is a choice, discuss it with your partner. How would the development of each conversation be different if no markers were used?

EXAMPLE

A: You can't be hungry again.

B: _____Well_____, you ate a lot more than I did.

A: _____Okay_____, that's true. Never again.

1. *Getting ready for a party.*

    A: Let's go over to the house and set up, all right?

    B: Um, set up. _____, first I need to get the sound equipment, and _____, actually I'll call Mike before I pick it up.

    A: _____, I'm gonna go, see if I have any messages.

    B: _____, see you there in an hour.

2. *Finding a place to live.*

    A: My new roommate left after a week. He goes _____ sorry, but my cousin has a cheaper apartment. Anyway, I'd much rather live with you.

    B: _____, actually the biggest problem, I think, would be my cat.

    A: Let me wait until I _____ talk to the doctor about my allergies.

    B: _____, then we'll think about it very seriously.

    A: _____, I may have to move out of my apartment either way.

    B: I will think about it, and I tell you, at this point it sounds like a good idea.

    A: _____, I hope things work out for us. Thanks for thinking of me.

3. *Making plans to meet.*

    A: If I go to Santa Barbara again, I'll call you and let's have dinner.

    B: _____, give me a call at work. Do you have my work number?

    A: _____, when I come out there again, I'll call you up if you're still there. It'll be _____ another year. We haven't been out there in a while.

4 **Practice conversation:** With a partner, choose one of the situations from the conversations in Activity 3 and create a new dialogue using the discourse markers *well*, *okay*, and *like*. Use each discourse marker at least once, and be prepared to explain the function of each one. When you are finished, practice your dialogue with your partner.

Situation: _____

A: _____

B: _____

A: _____

B: _____

A: _____

B: _____

Me too.
Incomplete Sentences

What have you learned from your grammar textbook?

Sometimes we give a **"short answer"** to a question. We **leave out everything after the auxiliary verb**:

A: Tom said he doesn't like pizza.
B: *Yeah, **he doesn't**.* [Omitted: . . . *like pizza*]

What does the corpus show?

A In writing, we usually use grammatically **complete** sentences. But many sentences in conversation are **incomplete**. These are not errors. Rather, there are particular times when we omit parts of sentences.

B **Minimal Responses:** Speakers use **simple words or phrases** to reply to what somebody else has said.

Minimal Responses		Function	Examples
fine	*great*	expressing **approval** of what the other speaker said	**A:** So Trey got the job? **B:** *Yeah.* **A:** *Great—oh, **nice**—that's wonderful.*
good	*nice*		
good job	*nice work*		
no problem	*thanks*	giving a **polite** response	**A:** *Thanks Deb.* **B:** *No problem.*
sorry			

C **Short Answers:** Speakers **omit subjects, verbs, and predicates** that **repeat** what the previous speaker said.

Omitted Form	Example
1. **subject + verb**	**A:** Where did you guys park? **B:** *Right over there.* [Omitted: *We parked* . . .]
2. **verb + predicate**	**A:** Do you have a couple of dollars? **B:** *No, **I don't**.* [Omitted: . . . *have a couple of dollars.*]

D **Shortened Clauses:** Speakers also **shorten noun clauses** that **repeat** what they have said or what a previous speaker has said. These shortened expressions usually **occur after particular verbs.**

Clause Type	Shortened Form	Common Verbs	Example
1. **infinitive phrase**	*to* only	*try* *want* *would like*	**A:** You don't have to fill the form out if you don't want to. **B:** *Well, **I would like to.*** [Omitted: . . . *fill the form out.*]
2. ***wh*-clause**	***wh*-word** only	*know* *remember* *wonder*	• I couldn't fall asleep last night—***I don't know why.*** [Omitted: . . . *I couldn't fall asleep last night.*]
3. ***that*-clause**	*so* instead of *that*-clause	*guess* *say* *hope* *think*	**A:** Have they found him? **B:** *I don't know—**I don't think so.*** [***so** = that they have found him*]

E Other types of short responses: Speakers may **omit parts of a sentence when the meaning is clear.**

Response Type	Examples
1. **question showing surprise:** *No kidding? Oh, really?*	**A:** I just go to school. **B:** ***Oh, really?*** [= *Oh, do you really go to school?*]
2. **fixed expression as question:** *What about . . .? How about . . .?*	**A:** How have you been? **B:** *Oh man, pretty busy.* ***How about*** *you?* [= *How have you been?*]
3. ***wh*-word as question:** *What? Who? Why? . . .*	**A:** Did you talk to Sharon? **B:** *No,* ***why?*** [= *Why are you asking?*]
4. **expression of similarity:** *so* and *too* substitute for the predicate	**A:** I'm running out of space here. **B:** *Yeah,* ***so am I.*** [= *I am also running out of space.*] **A:** I'm tired of books. **B:** *Oh,* ***me too.*** [= *I am also sick of books.*]
5. **compliment**	**A:** *Hi Will.* ***Nice shirt!*** [= *The shirt that you are wearing is nice.*] **B:** Thanks.

Activities

1 Notice in context: Read the two conversations. Underline the incomplete sentences.

1. *At a Thanksgiving dinner.*

MIKE: Delicious dinner, Ma!

MA: Thank you, but I had help.

SUE: I don't know who made what, but everything's terrific. Except the onions.

MA: Well, I didn't actually get to taste them, so I don't know.

MIKE: Dessert, anyone?

2. *After a work party.*

JEAN: Did all the men drive together in one car? I only see Dave's car over there.

ANNA: I guess so. I wonder why. They don't live near each other.

JEAN: Probably because Dave's really proud of that new car. He wants to show it off.

2 Analyze discourse: Look back at Activity 1 and at each incomplete sentence that you underlined. Write the phrase that has been left out. Draw an arrow between the incomplete sentence and the phrase. Discuss with a partner.

3 Practice the structure: The following dialogues contain some sentences that are too complete for natural conversation. Cross out parts of sentences that are too repetitive and write substitute expressions above them if needed.

EXAMPLE

MOTHER: Amanda, I'm your parent. I may raise my voice in discipline if I want to ~~raise my voice in discipline~~, but you will not yell back at me. I am very unhappy about what happened this weekend.

1. *Getting ready to drive home.*

   JENNA: I'm really tired, so I think I'm just going to start home now.

   BRETT: Are you alright to drive? You're not too tired?

   JENNA: I don't think I'm too tired to drive. I'll be fine.

2. *Talking about a trip to Japan.*

   JOHN: Did you get my postcard?

   DANA: Yes, I did get your postcard. And I was so happy.

   JOHN: That's good that you got my postcard. I told you I'd send you one.

3. *At the zoo.*

   BILLY: Wow, the zoo is packed. I wonder why the zoo is packed.

   SAMI: I don't know why the zoo is packed, but do you have more money for lunch? It's really expensive here.

   BILLY: No, I don't have money for lunch. Maybe we should go somewhere else to eat.

4. *At Erin's birthday party.*

   ERIN: Do you want something to drink, Tracy?

   TRACY: Yeah, I do want something to drink. Water'll be fine.

   ERIN: Melissa, do you want something to drink?

   MELISSA: Yes, I do want something to drink too. Some water, please.

4 **Practice conversation:** Work with a partner to provide logical responses to the following lines of conversation. Then complete the conversation on your own. Use at least four types of incomplete sentences. Then practice the conversation with your partner.

> *Making weekend plans.*

STEPHEN: What do you want to do this weekend?

MARIA: _See a movie or eat out at a restaurant. Whatever._

STEPHEN: Well, do you have the phone number for the movie theatre?

MARIA: _____

STEPHEN: I thought we could call and see what movies are playing.

MARIA: _____

STEPHEN: _____

MARIA: _____

STEPHEN: _____

MARIA: _____

The stuff I thought you could use
Complex Grammar in Conversation

What have you learned from your grammar textbook?

There are many kinds of **complex grammatical structures**, including (1) **adjective clauses** (also called relative clauses), (2) **noun clauses,** and (3) **infinitive phrases:**

1. Jack asked about the exam *that was scheduled for next Tuesday*.
2. Steve thought *the students were very smart*.
3. They wanted *to work harder*.

What does the corpus show?

A Compared to academic writing, the grammar in conversation often looks simple. Words and sentences in conversation are usually shorter and less complicated. However, **some complex grammatical structures** are actually **more common** in conversation than in writing: *that-noun clauses, if-noun clauses, wh-noun clauses, want + to-clause, thing/stuff + adjective clause*. The complex grammatical structures usually occur **after certain expressions**.

B *That-*noun clauses are common **after expressions** including one of these **four verbs: *think, guess, know, say*** (usually with *I* as subject, and *that* omitted—*see Units 31 and 32*):

Expression	Example
1. *I think / thought / don't think*	• *I think* I should put it back. • *I thought* it looked pretty cool. • *I don't think* he can speak Spanish. He can understand it.
2. *I guess*	• *I guess* you're right.
3. *I know*	• *I know* a lot of people do it.
4. *he/she said*	• *He said* he just gave up.

C *If-*noun clauses and *wh-*noun clauses are common **after expressions** including one of these **three verbs:** *know, see, wonder.*

Expression	Example
1. *I don't know if* *I don't know what*	• *I don't know if* you need one. • *I don't know what* I did with it.*
2. *I + modal + see if* *Let's see what*	• *I should see if* she's still there. • *Let's see what* we can do.
3. *I wonder if*	• *I wonder if* he still has them.

*See Unit 31.

D *To-*clauses are common after **one expression:** *I want to.*

• *I want to* go home.
• *I want to* ask you some questions.

E Adjective clauses are common as modifiers of the nouns *thing* or *stuff*, or indefinite pronouns like *somebody* or *something*.

Noun/Pronoun	Example
1. *thing*	• That was one *thing* I couldn't quite understand.
2. *stuff*	• I hate redoing *stuff* that's been done a long time ago.
3. *somebody**	• There's always *somebody* that you forget.

*And other pronouns—see Unit 43.

F Finally, it is common to find **several of the above expressions and nouns or pronouns combined** in the same sentence:

    • I don't know what *I want to* do.   • That's the computer **thing** *I think* I told you about.

Activities

1 **Notice in context:** Read the two conversations. Circle the expressions and the nouns or pronouns that introduce clauses.

1. *Decorating for an outdoor birthday party.*

    JAMES: Is there anything we can do with these decorations?

    BRENDA: I think we can easily hook the decorations on the tree. I wonder if I can secure it with a nail or something.

    JAMES: Right. What about the food? I wonder if we should keep the dogs inside so they don't get to it.

2. *About trying out for a school's volleyball team.*

    ANNIE: So, are you coming? Try-outs are starting in the gym today after school.

    CHRISTY: Volleyball's good. I think it's fun, but I don't know if I want to do it.

2 **Analyze discourse:** Look back at Activity 1 and at each word you circled. Write the type of clause that comes after each one (***that, if, wh-, to***, or ***adjective*** clause) in the margin. Draw an arrow between the circled word and the clause type. Discuss with a partner.

3 **Practice the structure:** Complete each dialogue with an appropriate expression from Sections B-E. There may be more than one possible answer.

1. *You and your friend Eric are talking about a trip.*

    ERIC: My brother just traveled to Denmark. He said he loved it. He said you're thinking about going, too.

    YOU: _____ go, but I can't afford the plane ticket.

2. *You are talking to Joe, your mechanic, about your car.*

    YOU: My brakes squeal when I stop. I think they're dying, but I don't have money to replace them. Do you think you can fix them?

    JOE: _____ what we can do. _____ if we'll have to replace them yet.

(continued on next page)

3. *You and your family are leaving for a vacation.*

YOU: I know you don't like to waste electricity, but can't we leave one light on while we're gone? Just to make it seem like someone's home.

DAD: _____ we can. It sounds like a good idea.

4. *Your friend Jeff is complaining about a homework assignment.*

JEFF: You know, I get so frustrated reading these old historic documents. I mean, it's like they're written in a totally different language. They're so formal! I can hardly understand them.

YOU: I have the same problem. _____ if we could find a more modern version of the text.

5. *You are talking with your friend Yoko after she returned from a trip to Peru.*

YOKO: When I was unpacking last night, I found a little lizard in my backpack, still alive. And I thought, how did a lizard get in there?

YOU: _____ it crawled in while you were camping.

6. *A father comes home early from a trip.*

DAD: Hey, I got in a day early.

MOM: Hi. Ooh, I know _____ that's gonna be happy to see you. (*holding up their baby*) Is that daddy?

4 **Practice conversation:** Carrie and Michael did not realize that the foreign film they rented had no English subtitles. Imagine their conversation as they try to figure out what is happening in the film. Work with a partner. Use as many expressions from Sections B-E as possible. When you are finished, practice the conversation with your partner.

Scene: *The film begins with a girl waving to her father as she stands on a quay. Her father is on a ship about to cross the Atlantic Ocean to America. He is going to America in search of a new life. In one hand, the girl is holding a large black leather bag. Her face is calm and happy. As she turns away from the ocean and walks back toward the city, the camera focuses in on her and then on a large white bird flying out to the sea.*

CARRIE: I **guess** she's happy that her father is leaving for America and a new life.

MICHAEL: I . . . _____

CARRIE: _____

MICHAEL: _____

CARRIE: _____

MICHAEL: _____

se   ,pecial Features of Conversation